The

CAT

The breeds, the care and the training

Grace Pond

With a foreword by
Beverley Nichols

BLACK CAT

Acknowledgments

All the photographs in this book are Orbis copyright with the exception of the following:

Crezentia Allen: 118, 119 – Animal Graphics Ltd: 141 – Camera Press: 10 – Walter Chandoha: 74, 85, 116T, 117T – Anne Cumbers: 14, 25, 30T (inset), 40, 50, 58/9, 68, 79, 81, 140, 143B (inset) – Mary Evans Picture Library: 9, 54, 86, 115 – I.G.D.A.: 64/5 – M. Orfini/I.G.D.A.: 15 – Photri: 75, 116B, 117B – Spectrum: 41 – Sally Anne Thompson: 12, 13, 26/7, 28, 29, 30, 38/9, 46, 60, 62/3, 66, 76, 80, 82/3, 90, 91, 98/9, 102/3, 105, 106, 107, 120, 121BL, 122, 123, 124, 126, 132/3, 134, 135, 136, 138, 139, 142/3.

Endpapers: Barnaby's Picture Library

The following writers also contributed to this book : Phyllis Lauder, Edwin Packer, Elizabeth Towe, Patricia Turner and Robert C. White.

Macdonald & Co (Publishers) Ltd,
3rd Floor, Greater London House,
Hampstead Road, London NW1 7QX

a member of Maxwell Pergamon Publishing Corporation plc

ISBN 0-7481-0010-5

Printed in Italy

Front cover photograph by Tony Stone Associates

Contents

Foreword

Because cats are the most beautiful of God's creatures—the most elegant, the most graceful, and of course the most mysterious—we should not fall into the error of regarding them through rose-coloured glasses. By all means let us write poems to them, and set them to music in the manner of Tschaikowsky, and pamper them, like the great Doctor Johnson, who ensured that his cat "Hodge" was supplied with a regular diet of oysters. But never let us forget that their exquisite bodies need scrupulous care and attention. An ounce of intelligence in this respect is worth more than a cartload of sentimentality.

Needless to say, there are some things in which cats need no instruction, particularly from human beings. Their standards of hygiene are far higher than those of the litter-bugs who deface our countryside. Their social sense is impeccable, and their poise, as they enter a room or descend a staircase, is worthy of study by the most accomplished professional model.

From these remarks you may gather, if you did not know it already, that I am more than somewhat fond of cats. Indeed the whole of my quiet domestic life vibrates to what might be described as a feline rhythm. Throughout every day of the year the cottage echoes to the sound of the little cat-doors, swinging backwards and forwards, as my three companions tabby, ginger and half-caste Siamese—go about their secret missions. In every corner of the garden you will find their signatures, scratches on the trunks of ancient trees. And occasionally you will also, I must sadly confess, find these same signatures on the carpets—only the softest, newest, and most expensive carpets, of course, for in these matters they have impeccable taste.

Yes, they have played, and always will play, a major part in my life, not only in care-free days of happiness but in times of great distress. The gentle warmth, the outstretched paw, the quiet music of a purr . . . these have an almost mystic quality of comfort, in which the animal and human kingdom are brought together.

No man will ever know *all* about cats. But this book will tell you most of the answers. And you will be the better for learning them.

Beverley Nichols

Classification of breeds

THE LONGHAIRS

BLACK
Colour: Lustrous raven black to the roots and free from rustiness, shading, white hairs or markings of any kind.
Coat: Long and flowing on body, full frill, and brush which should be short and broad.
Body: Cobby and massive, without being coarse, with plenty of bone and substance, and low on the leg.
Head: Round and broad, with plenty of space between the ears, which should be small, neat, and well covered; short nose, full cheeks and broad muzzle. An undershot jaw shall be considered a defect.
Eyes: Large, round and wide open, copper or deep orange in colour, with no green rim.

BLUE-EYED WHITE
Colour: Pure white, without mark or shade of any kind.
Coat: Long and flowing on body, full frill, and brush which should be short and broad; the coat should be close and soft and silky, not woolly in texture.
Body: Cobby and massive, without being coarse, with plenty of bone and substance, and low on the leg.
Head: Round and broad, with plenty of space between the ears, which should be small, neat and well covered; short nose, full cheeks and broad muzzle. An undershot jaw shall be considered a defect.
Eyes: Large, round and wide open, deep blue in colour.

ORANGE-EYED WHITE
Description as for Blue-Eyed White except for eye-colour, which should be orange or copper.

ODD-EYED WHITE
Description as for Blue-Eyed White except for eye-colour, which should be one eye deep blue and one eye orange or copper.

BLUE
Coat: Any shade of blue allowable, sound and even in colour; free from markings, shadings, or any white hairs. Fur long, thick and soft in texture. Frill full.
Head: Broad and round, with width between the ears. Face and nose short. Ears small and tufted. Cheeks well developed.

Eyes: Deep orange or copper; large, round and full, without a trace of green.
Body: Cobby, and low on the legs.
Tail: Short and full, not tapering (a kink shall be considered a defect).

RED-SELF
Colour: Deep rich red, without markings.
Coat: Long, dense and silky, tail short and flowing.
Body: Cobby and solid, short thick legs.
Head: Broad and round, small ears well set and well tufted, short broad nose, full round cheeks.
Eyes: Large and round, deep copper colour.

CREAM
Colour: To be pure and sound throughout without shading, or markings, pale to medium.
Coat: Long, dense and silky, tail short and flowing.
Body: Cobby and solid, short thick legs.
Head: Broad and round, small ears well set and tufted, short broad nose, broad round cheeks.
Eyes: Large and round, deep copper colour.

SMOKE
A Smoke is a cat of contrasts, the undercolour being as ash-white as possible, with the tips shading to black, the dark points being most defined on the back, head and feet, and the light points on frill, flanks and ear-tufts.
Colour: Body: black, shading to silver on sides, flanks and mask. Feet: black, with no markings. Frill and ear-tufts: silver. Undercolour: as nearly white as possible.
Coat: Silky texture, long and dense, extra long frill.
Head: Broad and round, with width between the ears, which should be small and tufted; snub nose.
Body: Cobby, not coarse but massive; short legs.
Eyes: Orange or copper in colour, large and round in shape, pleasing expression.
Tail: Short and bushy.
N.B.: The above is also the Standard for Blue Smokes, except that where the word 'black' occurs, 'blue' should be substituted.

SILVER TABBY
Colour: Ground colour pure pale silver, with decided jet black markings; any brown tinge

is considered a drawback.
Head: Broad and round, with breadth between ears and wide at muzzle, short nose, small well tufted ears.
Shape: Cobby body, short thick legs.
Eyes: Green or hazel.
Coat and Condition: Silky in texture, long and dense, extra long on frill.
Tail: Short and bushy.

BROWN TABBY
Colour and Markings: Rich tawny sable, with delicate black pencillings running down face. The cheeks crossed with two or three distinct swirls. The chest crossed by two unbroken narrow lines, butterfly markings on shoulders. Front of legs striped regularly from toes upwards. The saddle and sides to have deep bands running down, and the tail to be regularly ringed.
Coat: Long and flowing, tail short and full.
Body: Cobby and massive; short legs.
Head: Round and broad, small well-placed and well-tufted ears, short broad nose, full round cheeks.
Eyes: Large and round, hazel or copper colour.

RED TABBY
Colour and Markings: Deep rich red colour, markings to be clearly and boldly defined, continuing on down the chest, legs and tail.
Coat: Long, dense and silky; tail short and flowing, no white tip.
Body: Cobby and solid, short thick legs.
Head: Broad and round, small ears, well set and well tufted, short broad nose, full round cheeks.
Eyes: Large and round, deep copper colour.

CHINCHILLA
Colour: The undercoat pure white, the coat on back, flanks, head, ears and tail being tipped with black; this tipping to be evenly distributed, thus giving the characteristic sparkling silver appearance: the legs may be very slightly shaded with the tipping, but the chin, ear tufts, stomach and chest must be pure white; any tabby markings or brown or cream tinge is a defect. The tip of the nose brick-red, and the visible skin on eyelids and the pads black or dark brown.
Head: Broad and round, with breadth between ears, which should be small and well tufted; wide at the muzzle; snub nose.

Shape: Cobby body; short thick legs.
Eyes: Large, round and most expressive; emerald or blue-green in colour.
Coat and Condition: Silky and fine in texture, long and dense, extra long on frill.
Tail: Short and bushy.

TORTOISESHELL

Colour: Three colours, black, red and cream, well broken into patches; colours to be bright and rich and well broken on face.
Coat: Long and flowing, extra long on frill and brush.
Body: Cobby and massive; short legs.
Head: Round and broad; ears small, well-placed and well tufted; short broad nose, full round cheeks.
Eyes: Large and round, deep orange or copper.

TORTOISESHELL AND WHITE

Colour: Three colours, black, red and cream, to be well distributed and broken and interspersed with white.
Coat: Long and flowing, extra long on brush and frill.
Body: Cobby and massive; short legs.
Head: Round and broad; ears small, well-placed and tufted; short broad nose, full round cheeks.
Eyes: Large and round, deep orange or copper.

BI-COLOUR

Colours and Distribution: Any solid colour and white, the patches of colour to be clear, even and well distributed. Not more than two thirds of the cats coat to be coloured and not more than a half to be white. Face to be patched with colour and white.
Coat: Silky texture. Long and flowing, extra long on frill and tail.
Head: Round and broad with width between the ears which should be small, well-placed and tufted. Short broad nose, full cheeks, wide muzzle and firm chin (level bite).
Body and Legs: Body cobby and massive, short thick legs.
Eyes: Large and round, set well apart, deep orange or copper in colour.
Tail: Short and full.
Serious Faults: Tabby markings. A long tail. Yellow or green eyes.

BLUE-CREAM

Colour and Markings: To consist of blue and cream, softly intermingled; pastel shades.
Coat: To be dense and very soft and silky.
Body: Short, cobby and massive; short thick legs.
Head: Broad and round, tiny ears, well-placed and well-tufted, short broad nose, colour intermingled on face.
Eyes: Deep copper or orange.

COLOURPOINT

Coat: Fur long, thick and soft in texture, frill full.
Colour: (i) Seal points with cream body colour. (ii) Blue points with glacial white body colour. (iii) Chocolate points with ivory body colour. (iv) Lilac points with magnolia body colour. (v) Red points with off-white body colour. (vi) Tortie points with cream body colour.
Head: Broad and round with width between the ears. Short face and short nose with distinct break or stop. Ears small and tufted and cheeks

well developed.
Eyes: Large, round and full. Clear, bright and decidedly blue.
Body: Cobby and low on leg.
Tail: Short and full, not tapering. A kink shall be considered a defect.

BIRMAN

Body: Long but low on the legs. Short strong paws. Four white paws, the white on the rear paws to go up the back of the legs to a point like a gauntlet.
Head: Wide, round but strongly built, with full cheeks.
Fur: Long with good full ruff, bushy tail, silky texture, slightly curled on belly.
Eyes: Bright China blue.
Tail: Bushy (not short).
Colour and Condition: The colouring is the same as Siamese, Seal and Blue but face (mask) tail and paws are dark brown, in the seals and blue/grey in the blues. However, the beige of the coat is slightly golden. The paws are white gloved, this being the characteristic of the Birman cat.

TURKISH

Colour and Coat: Chalk white with no trace of yellow. Auburn markings on face with white blaze. Ears white; nose tip, pads and inside ears a delicate shell pink. Fur long, soft and silky to the roots; woolly undercoat.
Head: Short wedge; well-feathered large ears upright and set fairly close together; long nose.
Eyes: Round, colour light amber, rims pink-skinned.
Body: Long but sturdy legs medium in length; neat round feet with well-tufted toes. Males should be particularly muscular on neck and shoulders.
Tail: Full, medium length, auburn in colour with faint auburn rings in cats, more distinct ring markings in kittens.

THE SHORTHAIRS

GENERAL DESCRIPTION

Body and Tail: Well knit and powerful, showing good depth of body. Chest full and broad. Tail thick at base, well set, length in proportion to body.
Legs and Feet: Legs of good substance and in proportion to the body. Feet neat and well-rounded.
Head and Neck: Head broad between the ears; cheeks well developed; face and nose short.
Ears: Small, slightly round at tops, not large at base.
Coat: Short, fine and close.
Condition: Hard and muscular, giving a general appearance of activity.

BLUE-EYED WHITE

Colour: White to be pure, untinged with yellow.
Eyes: Very deep sapphire blue.

ORANGE-EYED WHITE

Colour: White to be pure, untinged with yellow.
Eyes: Golden orange or copper.

BLACK

Colour: Jet black to roots, no rusty tinge, no white hairs anywhere.
Eyes: Large and well-opened. Deep copper or orange in colour with no trace of green.

BRITISH BLUE

Colour: Light to medium blue, very level in colour and no tabby markings or shadings or white anywhere.
Eyes: Large and full, copper, orange or yellow.

BI-COLOUR

Colour: The patches of colour to be clear and evenly distributed. Not more than two thirds of the cats coat to be coloured and not more than one half to be white. Face to be patched with colour, and white blaze desirable.
Coat and Condition: Coat to be short and fine in texture. Body hard and muscular, giving a general appearance of activity.
Head: Round and broad, width between ears, which should be small and well-placed. Short nose, full cheeks, wide muzzle and firm chin (level bite).
Body and legs: Cobby with short straight legs.
Eyes: Large and rounded, set well apart, deep orange, yellow or copper in colour.
Tail: Short and thick.
Faults: Tabby markings, long tail, green eyes and brindling within the patching.

BLUE CREAM

Type: Body shape, head and eyes as for Short-haired cats.
Eyes: Copper, orange or yellow (not green).
Coat: Colours to be softly mingled, not patched, short and fine in texture.

CREAM

Colour: Rich cream, level in colour, free from bars; no sign of white anywhere.
Eyes: Copper or orange.

SILVER TABBY

Markings: Dense black, not mixed with the ground colour and quite distinct from it. Ground colour pure, clear silver, uniform throughout, no white anywhere.
Eyes: Round and well-opened; colour: green.

RED TABBY

Markings: Very dense and dark red, not mixed with the ground colour and quite distinct from it. Ground colour and markings to be as rich red as possible.
Eyes: Hazel or orange.

BROWN TABBY

Markings: Very dense and black, not mixed with the ground colour and quite distinct from it. Ground colour rich sable or brown, uniform throughout, no white anywhere.
Eyes: Orange, hazel, deep yellow or green.

SPOTTED

In judging Spotted Cats, good and clear spotting is the first essential. The spots can be round, oblong or rosette-shaped. Any of these markings may be of equal merit, but the spots, however shaped or placed, shall be distinct and not running into each other. They may be of any colour as suitable to the ground colouration. Colour of eyes to conform to coat colour.
Faults: Stripes and bars (except on face and head), brindling.

MACKEREL-STRIPED TABBY

Markings: As dense as possible, distinct from ground colour. Rings as narrow and numerous

as possible, and running vertically from the spine towards the ground.
Eyes: As for silver, red and brown tabby according to ground colour.

TORTOISESHELL
Colour: Black and red (light and dark), equally balanced, and each colour to be as brilliant as possible; no white. Patches to be clear and defined, no blurring and no tabby or brindle markings. Legs, feet, tail and ears to be as well patched as body and head. Red blaze desirable.
Eyes: Orange, copper or hazel.

TORTOISESHELL AND WHITE
Colour: Black and red (dark and light) on white, equally balanced. Colours to be brilliant and absolutely free from brindling, or tabby markings. The tri-colour patchings should cover the top of the head, ears and cheeks, back and tail and part of flanks. Patches to be clear and defined. White blaze desirable. White must never predominate; the reverse is preferable.
Eyes: Orange, copper or hazel.

RUSSIAN BLUE
Colour: Clear blue, even throughout and in maturity free from tabby markings or shading. (Medium blue is preferred.)
Coat: Short, thick and very fine, standing up soft and silky like seal skin. Very different from any other breed. (Coat is doubled so that it has a distinct silvery sheen.)
Body: Body long and graceful in outline and carriage. Medium strong bone.
Tail: Tail fairly long and tapering.
Legs and Feet: Legs long, feet small and oval.
Head: Short wedge with flat skull: forehead and nose straight forming an angle. Prominent whisker pads.
Eyes: Vivid green, set rather wide apart, almond in shape.
Ears: Large and pointed, wide at base and set vertically to the head. Skin of ears thin and transparent, with very little inside furnishing.
Faults: White or tabby markings. Cobby or heavy build. Square head. Yellow in eyes. Siamese type is undesirable.

ABYSSINIAN
Colour and Type: Ruddy brown, ticked with black or dark brown, double or treble ticking, i.e., two or three bands of colour on each hair preferable to single ticking; no bars or other markings except that a dark spine line will not militate against an otherwise good specimen. Inside of forelegs and belly should be of a tint to harmonise well with the main colour, the preference being given to orange-brown.
Absence of Markings: Absence of bars on head, tail, face and chest is a very important feature of this breed. These places are just where, if a cat or other feline animal shows markings at all, they will hold their ground to the last with remarkable pertinacity. The less markings visible, the better; at the same time the judge must not attach such undue importance to this feature that he fails to give due importance to others.
Head and Ears: Head to be a medium wedge of heart-shaped proportions, ears sharp, comparatively large and broad at base.
Eyes: Large, bright and expressive. Colour: green, yellow or hazel.
Tail: Fairly long and tapering.

Feet: Small, pads black; this colour also extending up the back of hind legs.
Coat: Short, fine and close.
Size: Never large or coarse.

RED ABYSSINIAN
The Red Abyssinian is the same in every respect as the Abyssinian except for colour, which is as follows:
The body colour is rich copper red, doubly, or preferably trebly, ticked with darker colours. Lack of distinct contrast in the ticking is a fault. The richer the body colour the better. A pale colour is a bad fault. The belly and inside legs should be deep apricot to harmonise. The tail tip is dark brown and this may extend along the tail as a line. A spine line of deeper colour is permissible. The nose-leather is pink. Pads are pink, set in brown fur which extends up the back of the legs. Eye colour is as for Abyssinians.
NOTE: As for the Abyssinian a white chin is undesirable: other white markings are not permissible.

MANX
Taillessness, height of hindquarters, shortness of back and depth of flank are essentials in a Manx Cat, as only with them is combined the true rabbity or hopping gait. The coat is what is termed 'double', namely, soft and open like that of a rabbit, with a soft, thick undercoat. Great attention should be paid to roundness of rump – as round as an orange being the ideal.
Remarks: Taillessness must be absolute in a show specimen. There should be a decided hollow at the end of the backbone where, in the ordinary cat, the tail would begin. The hindquarters in a Manx cannot be too high, and the back cannot be too short, where there must be a great depth of flank. The head is round and large, but it is not a snubby or Persian type. The nose is longish, but the cheeks being very prominent do away with snipyness, which is a bad fault. The ears are rather wide at base, tapering slightly to a point. Eye colour is of very secondary consideration, and must only be taken into account when all other points are equal. When that is so, it follows the ideal for the short-haired cats, namely blue for whites and amber or orange for blacks, oranges, tortoiseshells, etc. All colours of Manx are recognized, and here again, as in eye-colour, marking and colour must only be taken into account when all other points are equal.

BROWN BURMESE
Body Colour: In full maturity the body should be a solid, rich dark seal brown colour, shading to a slightly lighter colour on chest and belly. There should be no white or tabby markings. A few white hairs (though undesirable) may be permissible. Ears mask and points should be only slightly darker than the back coat colour. Top awards should be withheld from mature cats showing decided contrast between coat colour and points. In older kittens and young cats, all colours may be slightly lighter, with greater contrast permissible between coat and points. Young kittens will generally be lighter still, and may show tabby bars.
Body and Tail: The body should be medium in size, elegant, long (but not as long as Siamese) and svelte, and neck long and slender. Legs should be proportionately slim; hind legs

slightly longer than front and feet small and oval in shape. Tail should be long and slightly tapering. A whip tail is incorrect. An invisible kink at the extreme tip (although undesirable) may be permissible.
Head and Ears: The face should be wedge-shaped, but shorter, blunter and wider at jaw hinge than Siamese. The top of the head should be slightly rounded; profile should show a firm chin and a profile break at the top of the nose. Ears should be relatively large – wide at the base and slightly rounded at the tip. The outer line of the ears should continue the wedge-shape of the face. A jaw pinch is a fault.
Eyes: Eyes should be large, lustrous, wide apart, slanting towards the nose. The aim is for eyes of a clear, fairly intense, golden yellow, but the majority of the present-day Brown Burmese have eyes of chartreuse yellow. Really green eyes is a serious fault.
Coat: Coat should be short, fine in texture, and lying close to the body. A distinctive feature of Burmese is the glossy sheen of the coat, which is characteristic of good health.
Condition: Should be well muscled and carrying no fat. A Burmese cat has a typical firm feel when handled.

BLUE BURMESE
Body Colour: The body colour of the adult should be predominantly bluish-grey, darker on the back – the overall effect being a warm colour with a silver sheen to the coat – the tail the same colour as the back. There should be no white patches or tabby markings. A few white hairs may be permissible. Ears, masks and feet shading to silver-grey. Kittens are usually lighter in colour. Young kittens may show tabby bars.
Body and Tail: As for Brown Burmese.
Head and Ears: As for Brown Burmese.
Eyes: Eyes should be large, lustrous, wide apart, and slanting towards the nose. They should be yellowish green to yellow in colour, but really green eyes should be regarded as a serious fault.
Coat: Should be short, fine in texture and lying moderately close to the body. The characteristic glossy sheen of the Burmese is not so marked in Blue Burmese as in Brown.

CHOCOLATE BURMESE
In maturity the overall colour should be a warm milk chocolate: ears and mask may be slightly darker, but legs, tail and lower jaw should be the same colour as the back. Evenness of overall colour very desirable. Young kittens and adolescents may have faint barring and will be of a lighter colour. Nose leather a warm chocolate brown: foot pads a dark pink.

LILAC BURMESE
The coat colour has a faded quality, the general hue being a delicate pinkish dove-grey, with an overall frosted sheen. Legs and tail should be of the same colour, but ears and mask may be slightly deeper. Nose leather lavender or pink. Pads shell pink in kittens: adults may have lavender shading to pink, foot pads.

RED BURMESE
Rich golden red, shading to lighter colour on chest and belly. No spots or tabby markings except on face, but small indeterminate markings are permissible on an otherwise excellent cat. Ears should only be slightly darker than the back coat colour. Kittens may be lighter.

TORTIE BURMESE

A mixture of brown, cream and red, without any obvious barring. The colour and markings are not so important as the type, which should be excellent.

HAVANA

Havana Cats are of foreign type. They are fine in bone, lithe and sinuous and of graceful proportions. The coat is a rich brown, even and sound, whiskers and nose to be of the same colour as the coat. The pads of the feet are a pinkish shade. The eyes are green
Coat: Any shade of rich chestnut brown, short and glossy, even and sound throughout.
Head and Ears: Head long and well proportioned, narrowing to a fine muzzle, ears large and pricked, wide at the base with good width between.
Body, Legs and Tail: Body long, lithe and well muscled, graceful in outline. Legs slim and dainty, hind legs slightly higher than front legs. Paws oval and neat. Long whip tail, no kink.
Eyes: Slanting and oriental in shape, decidedly green in colour.

FOREIGN WHITE

The body should be lightly built, long and lissom, and the cat should have a well-proportioned and graceful appearance. The head should be long and wedge-shaped in profile and the face should narrow in straight lines to a fine muzzle. The eyes should be clear brilliant blue, and oriental in set; the ears, wide at base, large and pricked. The coat should be completely white, and the paw and nose leather pink.
Coat: Pure white, short, silky, even and close lying.
Head: Face narrowing in straight lines to a fine muzzle, in profile wedge-shaped with a strong chin; even teeth and bite; head set well on a graceful neck.
Ears: Large and pricked, with a good width between.
Eyes: Almond shaped and slanting, clear brilliant blue.
Body: Long and slender, the rump carried higher than the shoulders, well-muscled and elegant.
Legs: Long and proportionately slender; paws, small, neat and oval.
Tail: Long and tapering, whiplike.

CORNISH REX

Coat: Short, and plushy, without guard hairs and should curl, wave or ripple particularly on back and tail. Whiskers and eyebrows crinkled and of good length. All coat colours acceptable, but any white markings must by symmetrical, except in Tortoiseshell and white.
Head: Medium wedge. Head length about one-third greater than the maximum width, narrowing to a strong chin. The skull to be flat. In profile a straight line to be seen from the centre of forehead to end of nose.
Eyes: Oval shaped, medium in size, colour in keeping with coat colour.
Ears: Large, set rather high on head, wide at base, tapering to rounded tips and well covered with fine fur.
Body and Legs: Body hard and muscular, slender and of medium length. Legs long and straight, giving an overall appearance of being high on the legs. Paws small and oval.

Tail: Long, fine and tapering, well covered with curly fur.

DEVON REX

Coat: Very short and fine, wavy and soft, without guard hairs. Whiskers and eyebrows crinkled, rather coarse and of medium length. All coat colours, except bi-colours acceptable. Any white markings other than in Tortoiseshell and white will be considered a fault.
Head: Wedge-shaped with face full cheeked. Short muzzle with strong chin and whisker break. Nose with a strongly marked stop. Forehead curving back to a flat skull.
Eyes: Wide set, large, oval shaped and sloping towards outer edges of ears. Colour in keeping with coat colour, or except in Si-Rex, chartreuse, green or yellow.
Ears: Large, set rather low, very wide at base, tapering to rounded tops and well-covered with fine fur. With or without ear muffs.
Body, Legs and Neck: Body hard and muscular, slender and of medium length, broad in chest carried high on long slim legs, with length of hind legs emphasised. Paws small and oval. Neck slender.
Tail: Long, fine and tapering, well-covered with short fur.

SIAMESE CATS

SIAMESE (SEAL POINT)

Shape (body and tail): Medium in size, body long and svelte, legs proportionately slim, hind legs slightly higher than the front ones, feet small and oval, tail long and tapering (either straight or slightly kinked at the extremity). The body, legs, feet, head and tail all in proportion, giving the whole a well-balanced appearance.
Head and Ears: Head long and well-proportioned, with width between the eyes, narrowing in perfectly straight lines to a fine muzzle, with straight profile, strong chin and level bite. Ears rather large and pricked, wide at the base.
Eyes: Clear, brilliant deep blue. Shape oriental and slanting towards the nose. No tendency to squint.
Body Colour: Cream, shading gradually into pale warm fawn on the back. Kittens paler in colour.
Points: Mask, ears, legs, feet and tail dense and clearly defined seal brown. Mask complete and (except in kittens) connected by tracing with the ears.
Coat: Very short and fine in texture, glossy and close-lying.

SIAMESE (BLUE POINT)

The Standard is the same as for Seal-Pointed with the following exceptions:
Colour: Points blue; the ears, mask, legs, paws and tail to be the same colour. The ears should not be darker than the other points.
Eyes: Clear, bright, vivid blue.
Body: Body colour: glacial white, shading gradually into blue on back, the same cold tone as the points, but of a lighter shade.
Texture of Coat: The same as for Seal-Pointed.

SIAMESE (CHOCOLATE POINT)

The Standard is the same as for Seal-Pointed with the following exceptions:
Colour: Points milk chocolate: the ears, mask, legs, paws and tail to be the same colour, the ears should not be darker than the other points.

Eyes: Clear, bright, vivid blue.
Body: Ivory colour all over. Shading, if at all, to be to colour of points.
Texture of Coat: The same as for Seal-Pointed.

SIAMESE (LILAC POINT)

The Standard is the same as for Seal-Pointed with the following exceptions:
Eyes: Clear, light vivid blue (but not pale).
Body Colour: Off white (Magnolia) shading, if any, to tone with points.
Points: Pinkish grey, nose leather and pads faded lilac.

SIAMESE (TABBY POINT)

Type: As for Seal-Pointed Siamese.
Colour: Restricted to points as in all Siamese, basic Seal, Blue, Chocolate, Lilac and Tortoiseshell.
General Body Colour: Pale coat, preferably free from body markings and conforming to recognized Siamese standard for the particular colour of points.
Ears: Solid, no stripes. Thumb mark, except in the Tortie Tabbypoints, ears should be mottled red and/or cream as in the Tortie point Siamese.
Nose Leather: Conforming to recognized Siamese standard for the particular colour of points, or pink.
Mask: Clearly defined stripes, especially round the eyes and nose. Distinct markings on cheeks, darkly spotted whisker pads.
Eyes: Brilliant clear blue. The lids dark rimmed or toning with the points.
Legs: Varied sized broken stripes, solid markings on back of hind legs. In Tortie Tabbypoints some mingled red and/or cream patching on legs.
Tail: Varied size clearly defined rings ending in a solid tip.
Pads: Mottled in Tortie Tabbypoints.

SIAMESE (RED POINT)

Type: As for Seal-Pointed Siamese.
Colour: Restricted to points.
Body: White, shading (if any) to apricot on the back. Kittens paler.
Nose Leather: Pink.
Ears: Bright reddish-gold.
Mask: Bright reddish-gold.
Legs and Feet: Bright reddish-gold or apricot.
Tail: Bright reddish-gold.
Eyes: Bright vivid blue.

SIAMESE (TORTIE POINT)

Type: As for Seal-Pointed Siamese.
Colour: Restricted to points as in all Siamese: basic colour seal, blue, chocolate or lilac.
Body: As in equivalent solid colour Siamese.
Nose Leather: As in equivalent solid colour Siamese.
Mask: Seal, blue, chocolate or lilac; patched or mingled with red and/or cream.
Ears: Basic colour as in mask, patched or mingled with red and/or cream, which must be clearly visible.
Legs and Feet: Basic colour as in mask, patched or mingled with red and/or cream.
Tail: Basic colour as in mask, patched or mingled with red and/or cream.
Eyes: Blue, as in equivalent solid colour Siamese.
Coat: Very short and fine in texture, glossy and close lying.

Chapter I
Care and Management

Rearing a kitten

THE general condition of the kitten you choose as a pet should be self-evidently sound, with eyes clear, bright and shining and no dirt or discharge in their corners. The haws—the third eyelid which appears in the corners of the eyes in the form of a skin—should not be visible: if so, it is usually a sign of poor condition, and either the aftermath of an illness or the beginning of one. The inside of the ears should be clean, with no sign of ear mites that produce a condition generally referred to as canker. The nose should be cool and not running, while the inside of the mouth should be a healthy pink, the gums not red or swollen, and all the milk teeth through.

It should be gay, friendly, full of life, and not frightened and trembling when handled. It should be at least nine to ten weeks old.

However bright and lively the kitten, it may still be bewildered and shy on arriving at the new home. It should be allowed to explore the room at leisure, without con-

The kitten you choose should be gay, friendly and full of life, like the two here, who greatly enjoy being played with

stantly being picked up. A very small child should not be allowed to hold it, as small children tend to hug and squeeze young animals, often bending or even breaking the very soft bones. Before being allowed to nurse the new kitten, an older child should be shown the correct way to hold it, with one hand under the chest and the other under and around the back, so that the kitten feels secure. A kitten should never be picked up by the nape of the neck, as this may damage the muscles—a mother cat only carries a kitten this way when it is very small.

A low sanitary tray containing earth, peat or one of the proprietary litters should be ready beforehand. This should be stood on a large sheet of newspaper so that the contents are not scratched out all over the floor. On arrival, particularly if it has come a long way, the kitten should be shown where it is and taken there several times until it goes there of its own accord. If there is a garden, the tray could be moved nearer to the back door after a week or two, until eventually the tray is by it, and then later moved outside the door. The tray litter should be changed often, for cats are fastidious animals and will not use smelly trays.

The kitten should be talked to as much as possible until it gets to know its owner's voice. It should be nursed when it wants to be, given toys to play with, and not left alone too long. As kittens need even more sleep than puppies, a suitable bed in a draught-proof corner should be provided. This need not be an expensive bed or basket; most kittens settle happily for a small cardboard box with newspaper in the bottom, covered by a warm blanket.

Kittens have small stomachs, and three or four meals a day, about a large table-spoon at a time, is sufficient for them. Meals can consist of raw beef (this is an important item of diet), cooked beef, rabbit, chicken or lamb, kidneys, heart, tongue, any cooked white fish (with the bones removed), tinned sardines, salmon or pilchards, cooked or raw egg. Liver can also be given, but not too often as it may cause diarrhoea.

All the items in the above list should be cut up small or minced, because kittens have only their baby teeth until they are six or seven months old. Cornflakes or brown bread should be added to each meal. While the kitten is young, porridge, bread and milk, a baby cereal or break-fast cereal may be given as one or two of the meals. Some kittens are unable to tolerate milk, which may make the bowels very loose, but are able to take a little tinned milk.

Clean drinking water should always be available, and so should grass, a natural emetic. If there is no grass in the garden,

it should be grown in a pot or seed box. The kitten will chew the grass and thereby get rid of any fur that it may swallow and which could cause trouble by forming a hair ball in the intestines. A small dose of liquid paraffin or vegetable oil should also be given once a week as another precaution against this. Castor oil should never be given. Yeast tablets or a few drops of vitamin oil may be given daily. By the age of six to seven months the kitten's meals should be cut down to three in number, but increased in size. When the kitten is nine months, two larger meals a day should suffice, with perhaps milk at midday. The food should be given at regular hours.

After a few days in its new home the kitten should have learned to use the

sanitary tray. If it does make a mistake it should not be smacked or shouted at, but should be told 'No' very firmly. Attempts by the kitten to scratch its paws on the furniture must be firmly discouraged; if there is no garden with a suitable tree or a large log, a scratching post should be provided. These can now be bought at pet shops. The kitten must be taught that it is not allowed to climb on tables to steal food.

All kittens should be inoculated against feline infectious enteritis, a killer disease, when about 10 weeks old. Worming should only be done on the advice of a veterinary surgeon.

The eyes of the kitten are an indication of its state of health. They should be bright with no discharge in the corners

Caring for your cat

TIME goes by so quickly that all too soon the small playful kitten has grown up into a charming adult cat, but the care and attention it requires is still very much the same. Like humans, each cat has an entirely individual personality and, also like humans, cats vary greatly in intelligence, some being quick to learn and others much slower. All need affection and companionship. Nevertheless, the way any cat will develop depends a great deal on its owner.

For show purposes a kitten becomes a cat at nine months in Britain and at ten months in North America. However, if un-neutered, a male may be fully developed well before this age and may start 'spraying' (urinating on certain signposts of his territory). It is usually advisable to neuter it when it is four to five months old. A female may begin to 'call' (come into season when she gives the cry peculiar to her, that shows she is ready for mating) as early as seven months. Then she should be carefully watched to make sure that she is not mated at this age. If not to be used for breeding, the neutering of cats is advisable. It usually makes a cat more home-loving and ensures that, if a male, there will be no tom-cat smell about the house and, if a female, that no males are waiting hopefully outside, spraying all around the house and howling in the garden.

By the time the cat has become an adult, it should have been trained either to use a sanitary tray, which must be cleaned frequently, or allowed to go into the garden. It should realize that it must not scratch the furniture and, if there is no garden, be provided with a large log or a scratching post obtainable from pet shops. Climbing up the curtains should also have been discouraged by a sharp 'No' each time it is attempted, so that the cat will now appreciate that it is not allowed.

Even as a young kitten, the cat will have learned to answer to its name (when it wants to). It will have become a companion to his owner with a definite character of its own but a great deal does depend

Some cat lovers make the mistake of regarding milk as the staple food for their pet. A cat's diet should be varied. Too much milk (top) can be harmful; all fish (centre) should be boiled, steamed or baked. Tuna fish should not be given too often. Owners should set aside a short period every day for playing with their cat

Simple toys will keep a cat amused and provide it with necessary exercise (above and right). A scratching post (far right) should be provided, as scratching furniture is forbidden. A basket makes a comfortable bed for your pet (below right)

on its early training to ensure that it is a happy and contented cat, not a spoiled one.

Feeding at regular hours is essential, as is playtime and exercise, particularly if the cat is neutered, so that it does not become lethargic and fat. Simple toys, such as small balls, cotton reels and rubber mice, will amuse it for hours. Some cats learn to retrieve small pieces of paper rolled up into balls, bringing them back to their owners time and time again. Hide and seek is usually enjoyed, with the cat hiding behind and peeping out from furniture, or pushing coins under the carpet and finding them again.

As cats seem to spend a great deal of time washing themselves, some owners tend to overlook the fact that grooming is important, whether the cat is long- or short-haired. Brushing and combing will remove any dirt or dust in the fur and will also ensure that it is flea-free. If a pet cat is allowed to sleep on the best chairs, it is even more vital that it is kept as clean and healthy as possible; remember that fleas can lead to tapeworms and loss of condition. A fairly soft brush, with hair rather than wire bristles, and a suitable comb should be used. A steel tooth-comb is also useful should there be any fleas in the coat. It may be necessary to use a flea powder occasionally but the one chosen should be specially recommended for use on cats. Even so, it must not be left on the

coat for long but brushed out while the cat stands on a sheet of newspaper which can then be quickly picked up, trapping the fleas, and destroyed.

All cats benefit from gentle handling by their owners, and should be accustomed to this from an early age. It is important to know the correct way to handle a cat, since mishandling could result in injury. Never carry an adult cat by the back of the neck; the skin cannot bear so much weight and the muscles may be damaged. The correct way is to support the rear end with one hand, with the other hand under the chest. Only if the cat needs restraining should one hold it by the scruff, but the trunk must also be supported.

It is rarely necessary to bath a cat, but, if for some reason it has to be done, everything should be prepared beforehand. Bathing in the kitchen sink is best, as it is much easier to reach the cat at this level than when kneeling down to the bath. An inch or two of lukewarm water should be put in the sink and the cat stood in it, the ears being plugged beforehand with cotton wool to prevent water from entering them. The fur should be dampened *all* over and a suitable shampoo used – one recommended for cats or a baby shampoo. This shampoo should be gently rubbed in and then completely rinsed out, with a hand spray if available. Every trace of the shampoo must be washed out, otherwise the fur will feel sticky. The coat must be dried completely with a rough towel or with a hair dryer if the cat has no objection to the blowing and noise. The inside of the ears should be wiped gently in case any water has penetrated the cotton wool, and the corners of the eyes wiped. The cat

should be kept indoors until completely dry, as cats are very susceptible to colds and may easily catch a chill if allowed out too soon. If the cat comes in soaked after being out in heavy rain it should always be rubbed dry and when the fur is completely dried it can be groomed in the usual way.

The claws of a cat that does not get out a great deal on rough ground may grow extra long and in such cases it is advisable to get a veterinary surgeon to clip them as, unless great care is taken, the blood vessels may be cut, causing bleeding and pain.

An adult cat will require two meals a day, with clean water always available to drink, and also some milk, perhaps at midday, if it can be tolerated. Vegetable oil put down in a saucer may be licked up eagerly, or a dessertspoonful given once a week, and will help prevent fur balls forming. This may happen if the cat licks down quantities of fur when washing; if the cat is groomed regularly all the loose hairs should be brushed out. Grass for the cat to chew should be grown in a pot or a box, as it is a natural emetic and will also help to prevent fur balls. The Cat's Protection League sells seeds of a special coarse grass for only a few pence.

The food should be as varied as possible and may contain such items as raw meat (beef for preference), horsemeat (that fit for human consumption only), cooked chicken together with rabbit, kidney, heart or liver, all either cooked or raw. Care should be taken not to give too much raw liver which may cause diarrhoea in some cats. Fish, such as cod, hake, whiting or rock salmon, should be either boiled, steamed or baked. All the bones should be carefully removed. Tinned pilchards, sar-

dines, herrings or pink salmon may also be included. Excessive fish in the diet is inclined to cause eczema in some cats.

Cornflakes or similar cereals, or brown bread may be added to all meals to provide roughage and vitamins. Some green vegetables may also be given, if liked. Tinned proprietary cat foods are very useful but should not be considered as the main diet, as variety is very important.

It is not necessary to buy a special bed for the cat. A stout cardboard box, or a wooden one with half a side removed, with newspapers and a warm blanket in the bottom, makes very good sleeping quarters. The box may be renewed, in the interests of hygiene, from time to time. If a cat basket is bought it should be scrubbed and dried in the sun occasionally. The kitchen is usually the favoured place for the cat at night and if the cat is unable to go all night without excreting, a sanitary tray will have to be provided.

It is most unwise to put a cat out at night. Not only may it become involved in fights with other cats but it may cause an accident or be run over by a car and be injured or killed. If not allowed in the house at night a small shed in the garden with warm bedding and toilet facilities will ensure that the cat is not wandering around and is better both for the owner's peace of mind and for the cat. To be sure of getting the cat in at the right time, a favourite titbit could be offered each night.

All cats should be inoculated against feline infectious enteritis. There are several other serious illnesses which can also affect cats, for example, pneumonitis or 'cat flu'. This is curable but treatment must be started as soon as it is suspected. As the first symptoms are very similar to those of a cold, with running eyes and sneezing, a veterinary surgeon should be called in quickly – even if it is only an ordinary cold, no harm will have been done and early treatment may mean the difference between life and death. There are various other ailments that may affect cats, such as abscesses which often develop after a fight with another cat or even after an accident. There will be a hard, painful swelling under the fur, and the cat may go off its food and have a raised temperature. Hot compresses every few hours and a penicillin injection from the vet should reduce the infection before long, but care must be taken not to allow the wound to close and heal before all the pus has drained out. However, most cats live long and healthy lives and rarely need medical attention. Twelve years is normal, though some cats live for twenty years or more.

Cats are great conversationalists; many have quite a large vocabulary and an owner who really gets to know his or her cat soon recognizes what the various sounds mean. Various inflections of 'miaow' have different meanings. When food is wanted one sound is made, 'out' another, and 'in' yet another. Cats also have a language of gesture but this is very much an individual language and differs from cat to cat. Some cats learn to open doors, rattle door knobs and scratch at windows when they want to come in. They show affection readily, and will repay many times over the care and attention they receive from their owner.

The grooming of cats

ALL cats need some grooming, although many owners, particularly those with pet rather than pedigree cats, may feel that this is unnecessary, as cats are always washing themselves. Brushing the coat removes tangles, exposes parasites and scurf, cleans the coat and removes dead hair. It also acts on the skin, helping to keep it healthy and supple. Grooming should promote a healthy shine on the coat.

Cats moult once or twice a year, usually in the early spring and autumn, and brushing and combing daily will get rid of the old hairs. If not brushed out, there is always the danger of these being licked down into the stomach where they may accumulate, forming a sausage-like shape. Cats do regurgitate these from time to time. But if too much is swallowed, vomiting may prove impossible, as the hairball will form a blockage. The cat then becomes unable to eat, and this will mean loss of condition, and in extreme cases surgery at the hands of the veterinary surgeon. During the moult it is advisable to give liquid paraffin two or three times a week, rather than weekly, and to ensure that the cat always has grass to chew if it wishes, as this acts as an emetic.

Ideally, it is much better to spend some time each day on grooming rather than to have a weekly session. Naturally the time required will depend on the fur length, with Longhair breeds needing more attention than Shorthairs. Grooming should start at about three weeks. It helps the fur to grow the way it should, stimulates the circulation, and accustoms the kitten to being handled.

Condition is important. No matter how much attention is given to the coat it will never look at its best if the cat is not in tip-top condition. This means a well-balanced diet, no fleas in the fur, and no worms. The state of the coat reflects the health of the cat. While conformation and temperament are important in the eyes of the judge, a cat will be passed over at a show if it is out of condition or badly groomed. A cat which catches the judge's eye has a coat which is abundant, of a good texture, shining and well cared for. The skin, to support such a coat, has to be soft, clean and supple, and free from signs of parasites. Flea dirt can be seen in the coat as tiny, black, shining specks and, of course, the cat will be constantly scratching. The hair itself should be clean and resilient, without excessive moulting. If the coat looks lank and clinging it may be due to poor health and in this case the vet should be asked to advise. Systemic diseases have a detrimental effect on the coat and tend to make the hair fall out faster than normal. If a cat is unwell, it will stop cleaning itself, even the face, and so the owner must take over this task completely. Special attention to the paws and face is important at this time, and is an important contribution to the well-being of the cat.

The Longhairs need daily attention without fail, and even twice daily during the moulting season and if the cat is to be exhibited. Starting with the kitten, the frill has to be trained in such a way that eventually it will stand up around the head, forming a frame for the face. In the light-coated varieties, powder can be sprinkled well down into the roots of the fur and brushed and combed well out to remove the grease, but this is unsuitable for the Blacks and patterned coats. Before starting the grooming it is as well to stand the cat on a sheet of newspaper, as any loose hairs will fall on it, and can be burned later with the paper. Any tangles in the coat should be teased out with the fingers or with a thick knitting needle. If they are so bad that this cannot be done, they may have to be snipped off with round-ended scissors, taking care not to pull or cut the skin.

For the Longhairs, a brush with hair or nylon bristles is the best. Never use

Above: some people bath their cats before a show. It is very important to dry them properly. Below: a cat's ears should be carefully wiped out

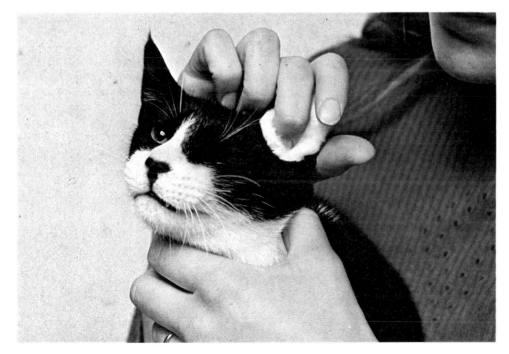

one with wire bristles, as these pull out too much hair. Two steel combs are necessary: one with very fine teeth for catching the occasional flea, and one with wide prongs that will go easily through the long fur. If many fleas are seen on the coat, a little insecticide powder (one specially made for cats) should be rubbed into the coat and then brushed out. Avoid spraying or powdering the face, as the eyes and mouth should not come into contact with the powder.

During the grooming session, and this applies to all cats, the ears should be looked at. If there is dirt, this may be wiped away gently with a little dampened cotton wool, but you should never poke anything inside the ears. A smell or a discharge may indicate the presence of ear mites, and the vet should be consulted for the correct treatment. If there is dirt in the corners of the eyes, this too should be removed with cotton wool. Some

Longhairs with very short noses and, indeed, other cats, do tend to get brownish matter in the corners which, if left unattended, will cause unsightly ruts each side of the nose. This should be seen to daily by wiping away with damp cotton wool, so that the face does not become permanently stained.

Powder must not be used on the dark coats, as it is exceedingly difficult to brush out completely, and any grains left look like specks of scurf in the fur. A little eau-de-cologne can be sprinkled down

Before a show, cats can be bathed as part of their grooming. They should be put in warm soapy water and dried very carefully with a rough towel or hair dryer, being kept in the warm until completely dry

into the roots, dried by gently rubbing with a warm towel, and the fur then brushed up. Eau-de-cologne will remove the dirt and grease, but great care is necessary to make sure it does not get into the eyes or mouth, as the cat will certainly object.

Many exhibitors of white cats, both long- and short-coated, bath them prior to a show. Bathing with a baby shampoo or a shampoo made for cats (as these are suitably mild) should be done several days before the cat is exhibited to allow the natural grease to return to the fur.

Grooming the short-haired cat is very much simpler as there is little tendency for the fur to mat. A soft brush, such as a baby brush, is ideal and a medium-pronged steel comb is necessary for occa-

sional use. Too-frequent combing may leave tracks in the fur. Comb the fur very gently, to avoid pulling the skin when tangles occur.

Generally, hard hand-stroking will remove the loose hairs and give the short, fine fur a good sheen, But some breeders advocate stroking with a damp rubber glove, an old nylon stocking or a suede glove, or with slightly dampened cotton wool. The coat can be finished by brushing it with a very soft baby brush, or polishing with a piece of silk or velvet, or a chamois leather which may be wrapped round the hand or the head of the cat's brush. Firm strokes in the direction in which the fur lies remove dust and make the fur shine. The Siamese particularly enjoy vigorous hand grooming from head to rump. Dead hair which collects round the rump can then be removed.

The Rex, those cats with wavy or curly coats, need slightly different grooming treatment. They do not have guard hairs and neither do they shed their coats regularly, as do other cats. A harsh brush must never be used on their coats. A soft baby brush is more suitable but, in fact, they need very little brushing or combing. Hard hand grooming, that is, stroking with the hands from the head to the tail, should keep the coat looking soft and shining. A light brushing with a baby brush will give the fur an extra sheen, and perhaps a comb through now and then with a very fine-tooth comb, to trap any flea that may have been picked up.

Cats can be dry-shampooed very effectively with bran. This should be preheated in the oven, rubbed well into the fur, and brushed out with a soft-bristled brush. Bran takes all the dirt and grease out of the fur and suits the long paler coats in particular.

The tails of some varieties can cause grooming problems, especially those of stud cats, which may become very stained and scurfy near the base. It is quite possible to wash the tail by itself. The cat should be sat on the draining board by the sink. A jug of warm soapy water should be made ready and stood in the sink. The cat's tail can then be put in this and thoroughly washed, rubbing gently where the scurf is. After several rinses, the tail should be dried and then brushed and combed as usual.

Some cats may be more difficult to groom than others, probably because their skins are more sensitive. In such cases it is far better to groom little and often, stopping when the cat starts to object vigorously. If grooming is started in kittenhood and the kitten is made an extra fuss of each time, it will look on grooming as a pleasurable routine, and will begin to purr when it sees preparations being made.

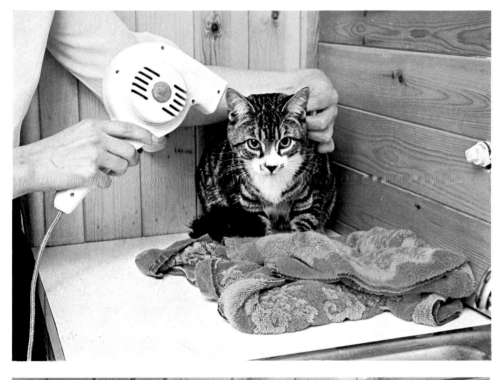

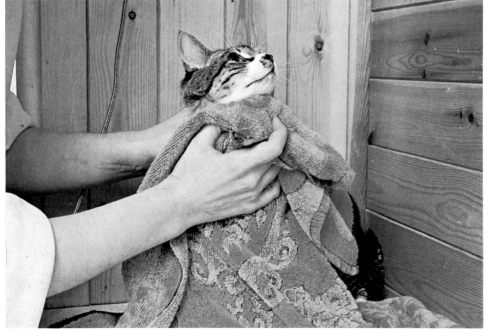

Common ailments of cats

THE majority of cats live long healthy lives, rarely being ill or in need of the veterinary surgeon's attention, but it is always wise to recognize symptoms of sickness so that any illness can be dealt with promptly. Fortunately, the most dreaded killer disease, feline panleucopaenia or feline infectious enteritis (FIE as it is called), is not quite so prevalent today, as kittens can now be inoculated against it.

There are a number of vaccines available and they can be in doses of one or two injections. The cat should be given the injection when it is about ten weeks old, but the vet will advise on this. Kittens and young cats are particularly susceptible to FIE, so it is most important that they are inoculated. The illness is caused by a minute virus and can act so swiftly that it may spread through a neighbourhood in a few days. Death can follow sometimes in a matter of hours, and poison is often suspected as the cause, rather than an illness.

The symptoms vary from animal to animal, but generally all food is refused, with the cat sitting crouched up, often over a bowl of water but making no effort to drink. There may be slight vomiting of a frothy mucus and the animal will show pain when the abdomen is touched, with dehydration following as the white blood cells decrease in number.

If the animal's life is to be saved, the vet must be called in immediately, as only swift treatment and constant nursing can save its life, and even this may not be effective. FIE is so infectious that the virus may persist on the premises for months afterwards, so all bedding used by the cat should be burned. The house should be completely disinfected and the owner should not visit anyone who owns cats. A new kitten should not be brought into the home for six months and even then it should have been inoculated beforehand.

Feline influenza or cat 'flu', also known as cat distemper, is another serious illness that can prove fatal to kittens and old cats. If it is treated in time, however, it may be cured with antibiotics and careful nursing. The symptoms are similar to that of a cold, with running eyes and nose, coughing and sneezing and a possible rise in temperature.

As there are a number of viruses which may cause 'flu', it has not been found possible as yet to produce an inoculation guaranteed to cure them all. Once the illness is suspected, medical treatment should be started, as there is less chance of bronchial pneumonia developing and more chance of a cure. There may be loss of smell and the animal may have to be tempted to eat with some favourite food, or force-fed with beef or chicken essence.

There are also a number of minor ailments which affect cats. They tend to develop abscesses after fighting with other cats, or from a rat bite. The owner may not realize this until he sees the cat sitting around, looking most miserable. Only

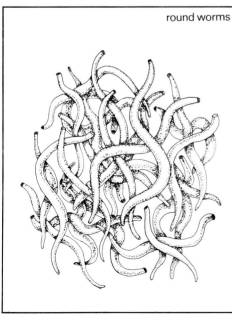
round worms

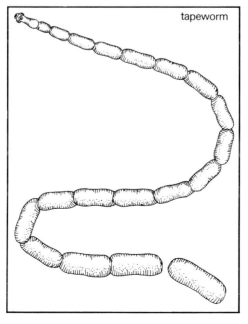
tapeworm

Above left: canker can cause a cat to scratch its ears and shake its head. A symptom of roundworms and tapeworms is poor condition; ringworm is a fungus infection

close examination reveals a hard swelling under the fur, which is obviously throbbing and causing great pain. The cat will go off its food and cry out when it is picked up. The fur should be clipped short and the abscess bathed with hot compresses every few hours. It is possible that, if taken to him early enough, the vet will be able to give an injection to reduce the inflammation but otherwise lancing may be necessary to allow the pus to drain away. Once this has happened the animal will be in less pain and should start eating. The abscess should be bathed frequently with a mild non-toxic disinfectant but must not be allowed to close up too quickly, otherwise it may break out again.

Diarrhoea can be the symptom of a serious illness or merely a stomach upset caused by eating fly-infected food, a change of diet or too much milk. Worms may also be a cause. To try to cure it, food should be given dry and only water given to drink. If the diarrhoea persists, veterinary advice should be sought. A cat may also suffer from constipation and this may be caused by too dry a diet or insufficient food. Castor oil must not be given but a little corn oil, liquid paraffin or sardine oil may help to correct this.

There are several skin ailments a cat may contract and, if bare patches in the fur appear, they should be examined very carefully. Without veterinary advice, diagnosis may be difficult in the early stages.

Eczema, which may appear as inflamed patches, can be due to an allergy or incorrect feeding, such as an excess of milk or fish in the diet. Eczema is not contagious but requires medical treatment.

Mange is not so common these days as it once was. It may have a similar appearance to eczema and is highly contagious. It is a very irritating complaint, causing the cat to scratch frequently. The animal should be isolated and treated professionally.

Ringworm is also very contagious and can be transmitted by the owner to the cat and vice versa. The first signs may be the appearance of what looks like cigarette ash in the fur and the appearance of typical round patches. This fungus infection was once considered incurable in animals, many being destroyed because of it, but fortunately antibiotics are now available which clear up the condition.

With cats any skin ailment should be treated with suspicion until a diagnosis has been made.

Fleas are often found in the cat's fur and, if they are not dealt with quickly and efficiently, they can cause tapeworms. A symptom of infestation is frequent scratching, particularly of the ears and neck, and the cat will suddenly turn and bite at its fur. Daily grooming and regular treatments with a flea preparation will

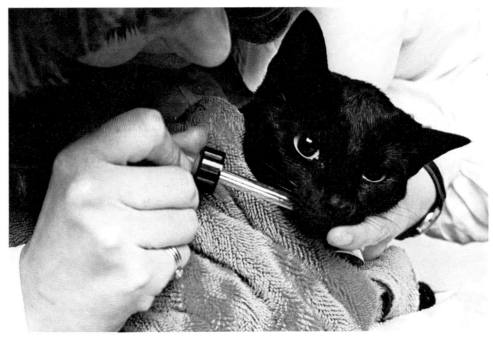

Above: (top) to prevent furball, vegetable oil should be given occasionally; (bottom) to give medicine wrap the cat in a towel and control the amount by using a dropper

solve the problem. It is also possible to buy an elasticated cat collar impregnated with a preparation lethal to fleas and which usually remains effective for three or four months.

There are two major types of worm which tend to infest cats: the round and the tape. Both require correct medical treatment. Kittens should never be wormed as a matter of routine, as an incorrect dosage has killed many a small kitten before now.

Tapeworms are the most serious, and can cause serious debility and loss of weight. The fur becomes harsh looking, the cat develops bad breath and has a

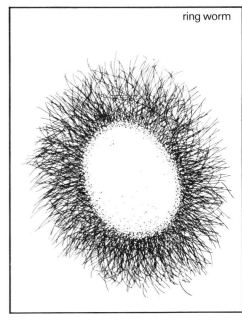

ring worm

22

This kitten is being inoculated against the deadly feline infectious enteritis

ravenous appetite one day and just picks at its food the next. The infestation may be caused by fleas acting as the intermediate host to the tapeworm, which attaches itself to the cat's intestines. Dried segments of the worm, looking like grains of rice, may be seen stuck to the fur around the anus. Correct drugs must be prescribed which will destroy the head of the worm and dissolve the rest of it. The dose should be repeated after two weeks or as directed by the vet. As there will be loss of condition, a tonic should be given for a few weeks and the cat put on an extra nourishing diet.

Roundworms especially infest kittens. The stomach usually becomes swollen, the fur lank and lifeless, the haws may be up and the kitten is listless. Worms may be seen in the stools looking like dirty white string. Here again, it is essential that the correct treatment should be given by a vet as quickly as possible.

Head shaking may indicate the presence of mites in the ears, commonly referred to as canker. The mites, which are too small to be seen by the naked eye, may be detected in the form of a brownish wax or a wettish discharge. There may also be a smell from the ears. Early treatment should be given if the condition is not to become chronic but a novice should never poke inside the ears, as they are easily damaged.

Cats catch cold just like humans and have running noses and eyes. A sufferer should be kept in a warm, even temperature, given a light diet and carefully watched in case the ailment is not a cold at all but the start of something more serious. Aspirin should never be given, as it has now been proved to be poisonous to cats, and can be fatal.

If a cat is seen to be straining, or appears to be in pain when passing urine and there are traces of blood in it, cystitis may be the cause. This is an inflammation of the bladder owing to a bacterial infection or a deposit in the bladder. Urgent treatment is required, for this condition has often proved fatal.

If a cat is groomed daily and has access to grass to chew (a natural emetic), any fur swallowed when washing should be either vomited or evacuated. Give your cat a weekly dose of vegetable oil as well, to help this process. If, however, the stomach appears to be swollen and your cat is salivating continuously, it is possible that the hair has formed a sausage-shaped mass in the intestines, a condition that will need veterinary attention quickly.

Another ailment found in cats, particularly elderly ones, is anaemia, which is a reduction in the normal number of red blood cells, or the concentration of haemoglobin in the blood, or both. This means that the oxygen-carrying capacity of the blood is diminished. General symptoms are pallor of the conjunctiva, gums, tongue, the inside of the ears and the nose. The cat may be weak and listless and, in very severe cases, may become breathless and lie on its side panting. Anaemia develops either from loss of blood, increased red cell destruction or decreased blood formation. Treatment of anaemia depends on the cause and the cat should be placed in the hands of the veterinary surgeon.

A cat may receive a wound from broken glass or a rusty nail, or in the course of a fight with another cat. If deep, the wound may have to be stitched; in any case it should be bathed with a mild disinfectant. The vet may consider it necessary to administer an antibiotic.

Dribbling and bad breath may be the symptoms of a bad tooth or tartar. Make sure the gums of teething kittens are not red and swollen. If they are, they will need the vet's attention.

To a sick cat, nursing may mean the difference between life and death. Cats can deteriorate very quickly and seem to lose the will to live when ill. Human companionship is vital; the cat should be encouraged and talked to cheerfully by the owner. Patience will be needed when giving medicine and when persuading the cat to take food. A sick cat can struggle with unexpected strength, so it is advisable to wrap it in a towel as if in a cocoon, giving the medicine through a dropper inserted into the side of the mouth. A drop only should be given at a time, to allow the cat to swallow without choking.

Nursing the ailing or injured cat

CATS have an instinctive need to be in the place they know. They will often return home after suffering an accident, only to collapse when they arrive. When they feel unwell they seek quiet, warmth and security, and this has to be considered when nursing a sick or injured cat.

An injury may leave a cat nervous and even unapproachable for a while after the event. Rest and warmth are essential, but examination and treatment are equally important. The cat should be placed in a basket or some other container which can be closed to ensure that it does not escape. If nothing else is available a large bag with a zip fastener is suitable. The owner should take care not to be scratched or bitten. If the cat panics or is extremely excited, a blanket can be thrown over it to subdue it for a few seconds and to allow you time to pick it up easily.

If a cat is so injured or frightened that it cannot be handled in any way, there are two things you can do. Leave it for a while and try again later. This is sensible where fright alone is involved but might be dangerous if the cat is injured. Alternatively, use a thick cord or a dog lead and form it into a lasso. The cat is caught by placing the loop over the head. Once caught, the cat should be quickly lifted into the container. Care must be taken to ensure that the loop is loosened as soon as the cord is released to ensure that the cat can breathe. Once in the basket the cat should be left undisturbed until seen by a veterinary surgeon.

There are things that can be done while waiting for the vet to arrive. If there is profuse bleeding use a tight bandage. If possible, dirt, glass or other foreign matter should be removed, and the wound cleaned with warm water. Broken bones are usually easy to detect. Do as little as possible in case there are other injuries. If you know that poison has been taken, act quickly. Make the cat vomit if possible, by giving it salt in water to drink. If necessary, pour it down its throat with a spoon or dropper, but be careful not to get the emetic into the lungs.

There are a number of general rules for nursing the cat after advice has been obtained. Keep the patient in a box or enclosed space that is large enough for the cat to lie fully extended and relaxed. This should be away from draughts and bright light. Some cats prefer a small blanket to lie on, while others seem to prefer newspaper. Whatever is supplied should be replaced when soiled. A dirt box should be placed within easy reach. Children should be kept away from a sick or injured cat.

The ailing cat requires more warmth than a fit animal. A constant temperature is ideal but this is often difficult to arrange. Hot water bottles are useful but they should not be made too hot. Remember that during the night the bottle will lose its heat. It is better not to provide one unless you are prepared to get up several times during the night to replenish the hot water, as a bottle that has become cold will do more harm than good.

Like a sick child, a cat often becomes unwilling to eat when unwell. Food should be appetising and nourishing, and should be given in small quantities. It is better to offer very small meals frequently than to provide a large amount of food twice daily, for much of this may be wasted. It is advisable, if all the food is eaten, not to give more for a while. Food not eaten must be removed. The sight of food constantly near the cat may reduce its appetite. If your cat will eat, care has to be taken to ensure that it does not become overweight. If a cat has a tongue injury or infection, food must be soft, palatable and without too strong a flavour. It is a good idea to vary the diet as much as possible if the cat needs to be persuaded to eat.

A sick cat may not be able to clean itself. This is a problem as when the animal is soiled, it feels uncomfortable, and recovery may be delayed. Unless advised otherwise by your vet, the cat should be groomed daily with a soft brush and comb. All tangles in the fur should be removed, the hair straightened and brushed into the natural position. Feet, ears and under the tail should be cleaned if they are dirty, using a little warm water.

When lying for long periods, cats should be gently picked up and turned to lie on alternate sides every three or four hours. This helps the blood circulation and prevents skin sores. Water should be available at all times unless this is against the vet's instructions. The cat should be prevented from licking its

An ailing cat needs a lying-in space large enough for it to be relaxed and comfortable. It needs more warmth than usual, so hot water bottles can be used (bottom) but must be kept hot. Licking of wounds is prevented by a collar (below)

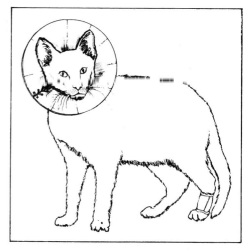

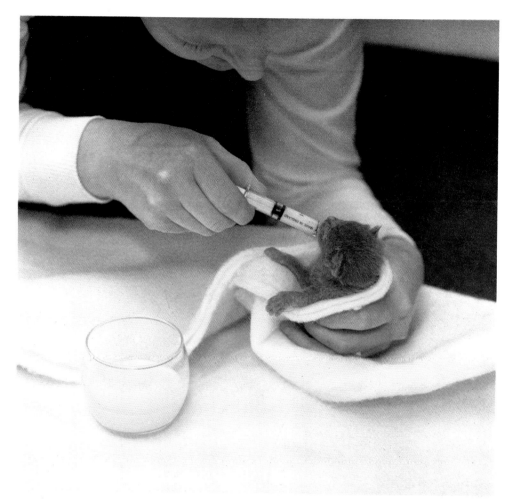

should not be poured directly down the throat, as it could go into the lungs.

Just like a child, an animal which has started to recover will try to do too much at first. Too much exercise, too much play, and overeating will all delay full recovery. Common sense must be used at all times when nursing an animal.

Naturally it is better to prevent injury or ill health from occuring, than to have to treat them. Make sure your cat is inoculated against Feline Infectious Enteritis. Keep it away from anything cooking on the stove. Keep waste pails covered so your cat cannot eat dangerous bones and the like. Screen high windows to protect your cat from falls. Keep all dangerous chemicals, poisonous insecticides and medicines in a cabinet. Keep lids on paint and varnish tins. Look in cupboards and drawers before closing them. Inspect washing machines and dryers, for cats can become accidentally trapped in any of these places. Finally, avoid using powders on the fur except for those made specifically for cats.

Remember that, throughout its life, your cat should be regularly handled and groomed so that, if trouble does occur, it will be used to being handled by you and will have confidence in you. This will make the treatment and convalescence much easier for everyone.

If the medicine is palatable the cat may lick it off a plate or spoon. Otherwise it will have to be given in a plastic dropper (above) or, if in tablet form, by using finger pressure to open the mouth (right)

wounds and sores as much as possible. In some cases, such as a head injury, it is necessary to make a collar which projects forward around the head, thus preventing the cat from scratching with its hind legs or from licking a wound on its body. A stiff Elizabethan collar can be constructed to serve the purpose. If the cat will accept such a collar it will recover much more quickly.

Give tablets by holding the cat firmly; press a thumb and finger on either side of the jaw to open its mouth. Put the tablet as far back in the throat as possible. Hold the mouth closed and stroke the throat to encourage swallowing. The cat can be firmly held by the scruff of the neck with the left hand, or held by someone else while you give the tablet.

If the cat will lick medicine off a spoon or plate, this is the best method of giving it. Otherwise, use finger pressure on one side of the cat's face to form a pouch in one cheek. The medicine can then be poured into this or placed there using an eye dropper (preferably of plastic, not glass). The jaws should not be opened. Give the medicine slowly. Medicine

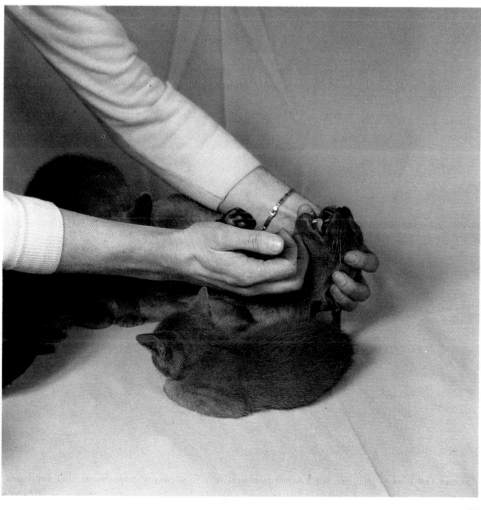

Cat language and communication

A cat is able to communicate better than most animals both with its own kind and with humans. Communication is not made only by sound, but also by gestures and facial expressions.

A kitten is able to express itself only a few minutes after birth. It purrs with satisfaction when first suckling from its mother and spits with fear or anger when sensing or smelling danger in the form of a human or a strange animal. It is born blind and is unable to see anything for the first week or two. When being weaned and first given raw meat, a kitten will growl quite ferociously at its litter brothers and sisters, definitely saying 'keep off' as they watch it with wide-eyed astonishment. In a very short time its affection will be shown by a closing of the eyes and a soft purring when it is being picked up and stroked.

A mother cat will converse with her kittens in a number of ways, using many different sounds and gestures. She will encourage them to follow her when they first start to walk, with almost bird-like chirps, using a deeper note as she becomes impatient with them if they ignore her. Another sound will mean 'come back' if they stray too far, which will become even more imperative if they take too long about it. There is also a very low drawn-out growl which definitely means 'danger–stay still'–for the kittens freeze into immobility when the mother makes it. She will purr with pleasure when the kittens are suckling, but after weaning has started and she feels it no longer necessary to feed so often, she will grunt and grumble, even shaking them off if they persist. If the kittens keep annoying her, she will box their ears, and stalk off with her tail waving furiously.

When they are first given a toilet tray, a gentle push with the mother's paw will start the kittens off in the right direction. She will mew at them encouragingly as they begin to realize what is required of them. She will show them how to wash by letting them see her lick her paw and then wash her face. Often they will try to copy her, falling over at their first attempts to balance on three legs.

From the fifth week on, this maternal behaviour towards the kittens declines and the kittens begin to take food from other sources. The mother tends to leave her kittens for longer and longer periods, and will actively avoid them at times. From the initial nursing stage, when the mother is suckling her kittens about 70 per cent of the time, this dependence gradually declines until by the fifth week she is only feeding her kittens about 20 per cent of the time. The weakening tie with the mother as source of nourishment takes place at the same rate as does the increase in movement from the maternal nest. The kittens begin extensive play activities both with their littermates and with their mother, but her annoyance at this and related avoidance of them probably plays an important part in the successful weaning of the kittens and their independence.

All cats are capable of a number of facial expressions. But each cat is an individual, and in time the owner learns to interpret the facial expressions of the individual correctly. A cat can express pleasure, fear, dislike, interest, boredom, amusement, and even superiority. Shutting the eyes when the cat is spoken to invariably shows that it is feeling pleasure, but sitting with them wide-open may mean astonishment or fright, although some cats sit and gaze at their owners for a long time when they want something, until they get it.

The way the ears are held is also indicative of a cat's mood. They are held high

In cats, the tail is an organ of communication with a language of its own; the pet owner gradually learns this language, as he gets to know the cat

Washing the litter is one way the mother shows affection which is returned by the kittens in the same way

when all is right with the world but, when flattened close to the head with the eyes mere slits, this is most definitely a danger signal. A flick of the ears when called means 'I hear you but choose to ignore you'.

The paws, too, are used as a method of communication, being kneaded up and down with pleasure and employed as weapons of defence, with claws at the ready, if the cat is attacked. They are also used to show the cat's affection when it gently pats the owner's cheeks with them. A cat will show its dislike of whistling by coming and putting a paw on the owner's mouth for silence.

The tail will be moved lazily from side to side when the cat is happy with the world, but it may be lashed violently around to show extreme annoyance; a twitching of the tip alone may mean anger. An arched back, with the fur on end, and the cat standing stiff-legged, is a warning. It acts as a deterrent (which few choose to ignore) to most dogs meeting a strange cat.

The cat vocabulary is a large one, but cats differ considerably in the way they converse. The foreign varieties, such as the Siamese, are usually the most vocally communicative. The amount of conversation depends a great deal on the interest the owner shows in the cat. Cats are very polite and invariably answer when spoken to. The length and tone of the sounds made by cats vary according to the meaning they wish to express. If a cat is very hungry and the meal is late, the cry will be short and demanding, with perhaps a pawing. A 'want out' mew at the door is one that most owners soon learn to understand and also the polite little 'thank you' when the door is opened. It may take a new owner some time to sort out what the various sounds made by their pet mean. There will be a howl of anguish when it is hurt, a plaintive cry when it has been ignored for too long, a cheerful mew given when passing the time of the day with the owner or a friendly cat, and a 'battle cry' when sighting an enemy. And during mating time there is yet another, indescribable yowling noise made by the female cat when in season, and the caterwauling of the tom-cat seeking a female. The mating calls are also heard during copulation itself.

Jealousy is shown by growling, glaring and lashing of the tail, while turning of the back and walking away mean aloofness from a situation. Spitting and hissing mean dislike and 'beware', while purring, which appears to be done involuntarily, is indicative of pleasure. Some cats have very quiet mews, opening their mouths and making very little sound at all, but the very way they do this will still manage to convey a message to their owners, if they have an understanding of their pets.

The way a cat washes itself can also convey its mood. A long leisurely wash means that it is relaxed, while sitting down and starting to wash when the owner is calling it is a clear way of indicating complete indifference. A wash with short, sharp angry licks means 'watch out'. This is often done when an unknown cat is approaching, which also then sits down to wash; both are waiting for the other to make the first move. Whatever the gesture or sound used, a cat is certainly not a dumb animal but one that can converse most adequately in very many ways, given complete understanding on the part of its owner.

So far, communication by gesture, facial expression and sound has been dealt with as a means of making known the cat's needs and emotions to humans and other cats. In the animal world there are, of course, other methods of conveying a message, much as in the human world there are other means than speech of giving information. Just as humans erect notices 'Private property: keep out' or

'Trespassers will be prosecuted', so in the animal world there are means whereby an animal can inform others of the same species that they are on its territory.

The male cat is particularly concerned about territorial rights. He will take over an area of the garden or ground surrounding the house and will fight all other male cats that come inside the perimeter. He also has an instinct to try and increase the size of his territory. Other cats are made aware of this territory because it is marked out by the smell of the tom-cat's urine. Every male cat has its own distinctive urine smell; this is left around the boundary of the territory after the cat has urinated against trees, fences, posts and walls. The smell lasts for several days and when it shows signs of fading the male cat will re-mark his territory in the same way. Unfortunately for the owners of tom-cats that have not been neutered (had certain sex organs removed), some male cats adopt the house as their territory, and will spray the strong-smelling urine on curtains, furniture and walls. This is really a most unpleasant smell for all but the most devoted of cat-lovers, and it takes a long time to clear. There is always the possibility, if not the certainty, that the male cat will repeat the operation inside the house even though you show your displeasure, because this spraying of territory is an instinct which is extremely hard to suppress once the habit has started.

For this reason, most cat breeders do not allow the male cat to live in the house, but provide him with a sturdy stud house in the garden or grounds. It should be said that there are exceptions to this rule; there are male cats that never spray inside the house, but usually they are cats that live in rural surroundings and have a large expanse of countryside that they can claim as their territory. This marking of territory in mammals is related to the sexual activities of the animals concerned. It is interesting to note that other mammals have similar ways of marking territory. Bears and bison, for example, roll in their urine so that their hides are impregnated with it, and then they rub it off on certain trees in their territory. The male hippopotamus uses a mixture of urine and dung to mark his area and to warn off any of his rivals.

There are instances of communication that warn others in the same pack or group of lurking danger. Some fishes, such as minnows, when bitten by a predator fish give off a substance into the water which other minnows in the shoal recognize through a sense of smell. Such a smell tells them that a predator is in the vicinity and they immediately take flight. But the domestic cat is not a pack animal, so it does not possess a means of warning others of danger, only of showing that it is aware of danger itself.

If one had to chose a breed of cat in which communication by facial expression is most clearly expressed, then perhaps those with tabby markings would be selected. This is the view put forward by Konrad Lorenz, the world-famous animal psychologist. He acknowledges that the face of a cat can display unmistakably the slightest degree of agitation to anyone who knows the animal well. To catch the slightest movement of the facial skin is much easier if one is looking at a cat with striped markings similar to the wild cat. 'The slightest vestige of mistrust', says Lorenz, 'and the innocent round eyes become somewhat almond shaped and oblique, and the ears less erect; and it requires neither the subtle change of bodily attitude nor the gently waving tip of the tail to inform the observer that the mental state of the animal is undergoing a transition.'

Cat owners who study their cats know this only too well. In time the cat lover becomes sensitive to every change in the cat's bearing and facial expression. Cats lack speech, indeed, and yet they find ways of telling us everything they want us to know!

Arching the back, fur on end, and legs straight and tense, is a warning to dogs and strange cats to keep their distance

Anatomy of the cat

THE body of the cat is designed for self-preservation. Indeed, the old saying that cats have nine lives is based on the observation that they seem to possess a great ability to survive injury in circumstances where other animals would be severely harmed or even killed. Quite apart from this they have beauty, strength and intelligence.

In the wild state the cat is a solitary hunter with an independent nature. Unlike the dog, whose domestication has resulted in its being dependent on humans, cats can fend for themselves, find food, warm shelter and keep themselves clean, if for any reason this becomes necessary. The cat–like the dog–becomes attached both to people and a home but, if choice has to be made, will always choose to remain with its owner. When a move takes place the cat will soon adjust to its new surroundings.

Many owners are worried at the thought of moving a cat to a new house. The secret is to ensure that the cat becomes familiar with the new surroundings. Once this is done it is relatively easy to put a cat outside the house when food is ready and call it in for the meal–by doing this the cat learns where its new house is in relation to the garden and so adopts the garden as its new territory. In other words, it learns to find its way home.

The ability to survive is partly a result of the cat's anatomy. The bones of the shoulder are so shaped that a cat is able to wrap its forelegs around a tree and climb with ease. If you watch a kitten playing you will see that it can move its legs in almost any direction. The end of the ribs do not harden as quickly as in other animals, and this enables a cat to withstand more pressure on the chest.

We all know that cats are essentially tree-climbers and like to sit on a raised object. This may be a chair, the top of an out-building or a fence. This allows them to survey their surroundings in case of approaching danger. Their sense of balance is good, their reflexes extremely fast. They can change from a relaxed state to an alert one in a flash.

Few animals are more graceful both at rest and in movement than the cat. In spite of many thousands of years of domestication, the cat retains the agility and grace of its ancestors. It can accelerate swiftly, and can become motionless almost as quickly. It has a number of gaits; there is the dignified walk, the loping canter and–when prey is sighted and the time for attack has come–an explosive leap forward. The muscles of the hind-

quarters are powerful, and this gives it an impressive momentum when moving towards a tree it wishes to climb. This momentum is transferred from the horizontal to the vertical as the tree is reached. Then the claws come into play, enabling the cat to keep its hold.

The claws are retractable so that a cat can creep softly when hunting but can bring them into instant aggressive use if needed. They grow continuously and, if not worn down, become uncomfortable, in which case the cat sharpens and shortens them by clawing at wood or other substances. This can become a problem when a cat is kept in a flat or where exercise is limited, as the furniture, or even a carpet, may be used for this purpose. The provision of a piece of wood as a 'scratching block' may solve this problem, or the nails can be cut. If the latter method is used care must be taken to ensure that the blood vessel in the upper part of the nail is not severed.

The eye is adaptable. The pupil is able to expand to twenty times its smallest size and so the cat can make the maximum use of extremely diffuse light. The ability to 'see' at night is assisted by the whiskers, and the long hairs that make up the eyebrows and occur on the end of the ears. These are very sensitive and enable the cat to feel its way about even in darkness.

It is not only the eye and sense of touch that are well developed: so too is the sense of hearing. Cats can hear sounds that we cannot. This is for two reasons: firstly their hearing is more acute; secondly, they have the ability to appreciate sounds that are too high for the human ear to distinguish. It is believed that a cat's hearing is more acute than a dog's. This is aided by the cat's erect ears which help to collect the incoming sounds. Twenty muscles control these ear flaps and enable them to be rotated towards sounds, thus increasing the cat's hearing ability and enabling it to position the source of the noise accurately.

Just as the anatomy of the cat is adapted for survival, so is its physiology. Fear in all animals stimulates the production of adrenalin, which in turn causes many changes to occur. In a cat these changes can be seen by the sudden alteration in shape of the animal. The coat stands on end, the tail hairs bristle, the tail itself becomes stiffened, the back arches and the legs are held straight. All these make the cat appear larger, and thus are intended to frighten any attacker.

The feline body is particularly sensitive to certain drugs and even to food. Some

cats appear to be unable to digest milk, while many normal cats, if fed with moist food, rarely drink because they have the ability to conserve water. Where this occurs it is usually a sign of health. Other cats do drink, and so if a cat always drinks approximately the same amount of water each day this can be considered normal. It is only when a marked change in the drinking habits occurs that trouble should be suspected. As with all animals, water should be available at all times.

Milk has the effect of loosening the bowels of some cats, even causing diarrhoea. Fortunately it is not essential for cats to have milk–this is an old wives' tale–and other dairy products can be substituted, such as cheese or butter. Cats are individualists: some like buttered toast with a yeast spread such as Marmite, some like toasted cheese. Every cat owner must study his pet and find out just what its food likes and dislikes are. Essentially the cat must have a varied diet, for if you restrict it to the items it obviously likes, that diet may be deficient in certain nutritional components. The effect of this deficient diet will not reveal itself for some considerable time, possibly several months, and the owner may not think that the food he is providing could be the cause of the cat's illness or disorder when it arises. Certain dried cat foods are a complete diet, but if you do not use these–and the cat may show a disinclination to eat them–it a good idea to add a vitamin-mineral supplement to your pet's food.

Fish, if eaten in excessive quantities, can lead to certain skin conditions. In the same way, excessive liver in the diet can lead to too much vitamin A being absorbed, with a resulting possibility of arthritis of the spine. Excessive fat will hinder the absorption of vitamin E and this in turn leads to the development of the so-called yellow fat disease of cats.

However, it is not just food that has to be supplied in suitable proportions. Where preservatives are used in the food, these must also be controlled. Recently it has been found that too much benzoic acid used for this purpose can lead to symptoms of nervousness in cats.

Such a finely adjusted body can create problems. When ill health occurs, some

Left: the claws of a cat grow continuously, so that the cat must shorten and sharpen them on trees or other surfaces. Inset, top: a cat's fast reflexes allow it to be completely relaxed at one moment and on the alert the next. Inset, below: the thick, sensitive whiskers aid perception

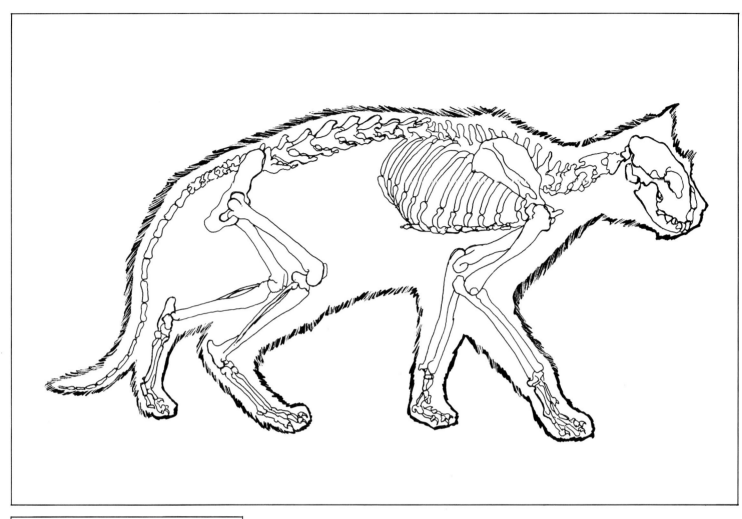

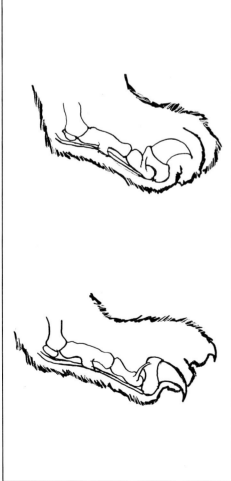

cats will just try to 'sleep it off'. Others, notably the Siamese and Burmese seem to feel that the end of the world has come when they are ill and appear to lose the will to live. Such changes in the cat's normal behaviour are a sign that expert advice should be obtained. Home treatment can be dangerous; for example, aspirin can be fatal if given to a cat.

But even when expert advice is obtained and acted upon, the cat's owner still has a big part to play in the nursing of the ailing cat. When they are unwell, cats come to rely a great deal on human sympathy and understanding. At times like these, some of their sturdy independence is lost. If the illness is really serious, then you may have to sit with the cat all night, just as you would with a sick person. Many breeders have a special sick room, and sleep there on a camp bed beside the sick cat, so that they can always be at hand when needed. During the night the cat can be reassured of your presence in a number of little ways – talking to it, wiping away mucus from nose and mouth, seeing that it does not get too hot or chilled – and this constant care undoubtedly helps in giving the cat a will to live. Even your tone of voice can have an effect on the cat; cats are quick to notice these things, so always talk to it in a cheerful voice, never a doleful one.

The skeleton of the cat (above) is designed for speed, agility and flexibility. Left: a cat's claw is normally kept retracted for walking (above), but can be brought into use quickly (below)

Cats enjoy life best when it is interesting and varied. They will, if allowed, go and catch a meal rather than eat what they are given if they feel that this is not to their liking. This independence is proverbial and is possibly their chief attraction. They are all individuals.

All cats have their likes and dislikes. The idea that they dislike getting wet is incorrect. Some do, but others enjoy playing with water; they may play with a hose, paddle in a stream or pond or go fishing.

Cats have a language and use it to communicate with humans. If they ask for a door to be opened the call is readily understood. And they do not forget their manners – they always give a small miaow to say 'thank you' when the door is opened. They purr when happy. They miaow, but only to humans, not to other cats. The cat owner is trained by the cat to know what his pet is wanting, and is also rewarded by praise when the lesson is learnt. Some pet-lovers believe that the most subtle difference between the dog and the cat is that the owner trains the dog while the cat trains the owner.

Sexual activities in cats

FEMALE cats develop physically at different ages, but six months is generally considered to be the average age at which a female cat (or queen) may come into season for the first time. It may be a little earlier in some of the Foreign Shorthairs and later in the Longhairs. Coming into season is also referred to as 'oestrus', 'calling' or 'on heat'. A cat should not be mated at this early age, as she will not yet be fully grown and if mated, will invariably lose the kittens. Great care should be taken to ensure that the female does not get out when calling or she may be mated by a stray. Ten months is young enough for the first mating and only then if she has already called at least once before this.

The mating or oestral cycle of the majority of female cats is unpredictable, although after a while some owners are able to work out approximately when a female may be expected to come into season, and so book her with a stud well in advance. Unlike a dog that comes into season only twice a year, a cat may call every month between February and early October. Of course, there are exceptions to this, with some cats calling in November, December and January as well, while others may only call once or twice during the whole season.

Not all are noisy callers, some show few signs apart from extra friendliness. With such cats it may be difficult to know when they are ready for mating, and perhaps only when the owner notices that the animal has increased in bulk will it be realized that she is in fact in kitten and has already called.

The first stage of calling is known as the pro-oestrous period, when close examination may show a slight swelling of the vulva, with the cat becoming very affectionate and possibly eating more. The majority of females do give fair warning and, as the true period of the oestrus starts, refuse to leave their owners alone. They demand attention all the time, becoming more restless, sometimes going to the window looking for a mate, trying to get out and eating very little. There may be rolling on the floor, padding up and down with the back legs, frequent mewing and muttering, and often loud howling. Although this may be frightening, the cat is not in pain, but her howls may get louder and louder, owing to sexual frustration. Further examination will show that the vulva is now more swollen, and there is a slight discharge. It may be difficult to notice the discharge as the cat will invariably lick this away, but if watched it will be evident that she is washing there much more frequently than usual. She may leave a slight pinkish droplet around, but this does not always happen, and no special hygienic arrangements are necessary.

The length of the call varies from cat to cat. In some it may last only two or three days, while with others it may go on for as long as ten days. Some queens call again and again, almost without cease, until the owner, in desperation, although not really wanting her to have kittens, sends her away to be mated. If a female is not re-

Studs are kept outside once they start to spray because of the offensive smell

quired for breeding, it is advisable to have her neutered as soon as the veterinary surgeon considers she is old enough, which will probably be when she is about four-and-a-half months old.

Most stud owners like the queen to be sent to the stud on the second day of the full oestrous period. Experience has shown that the stud cat's advances are accepted more readily on the third day. Although males are capable of mating at any time, once fully developed, the females can only be mated when calling, and some—particularly the nervous ones—stop when brought to the stud and have to make a return visit.

It is possible for a queen, even if not mated, to have a false pregnancy, and to show all the signs of being in kitten, with ever-increasing bulk and milk in the breasts. When the date of the supposed kittening has passed, the cat starts to decrease in size, eventually becoming her normal self. Some queens, on examination, prove to be definitely in kitten and increase in size, but as weeks pass, nothing happens and no kittens arrive, and the cat reverts to her normal size. It is thought that in these instances, although successfully mated, the cat will have absorbed the kittens, and yet may be none the worse. But it is advisable, should this have happened, to let the vet examine her afterwards to make sure all is well.

Occasionally, when in season, a female cat may start to spray around like a tom, and a close watch should be kept for this. There is a smell, but it is not nearly so pungent as that of the male. Also, when calling, although usually very clean and house-trained, a queen may become dirty and start to urinate in the house, but she will resume good behaviour once the oestrous cycle is over.

Spraying is a term invariably associated with the male or tom-cat. A male cat is able to emit a fine spray of urine at will. By raising the tail, he is able to direct the spray from the penis backwards at specific objects, including, if allowed indoors, curtains and furniture. This urine has a highly pungent smell, offensive to most people, and is the main reason why it is usually quite impossible to keep a fully matured male in the house as a pet. If not to be used as a stud, a male should be castrated well before it reaches sexual maturity, otherwise the habit of spraying may continue in a neuter.

Spraying as such is not the same as the cat passing urine in the normal squatting manner. Once a tom-cat has started this habit, it appears to be impossible to train it not to spray in the house. There are a few exceptions, with full males that never spray indoors. Some stud owners have found that it is possible to have a male in the house in the winter time when there are no calling females about, but a careful watch always has to be kept on it.

If a tom-cat is not to be used as a stud, it is advisable to have it neutered when it is old enough. Males do not usually start spraying until they have reached full adulthood and some do not start this habit until two years old or more. Once they have been used as studs, they start spraying. The process is probably one way of letting the female cats know that a male is around, and also a form of territorial behaviour, allowing other males to know the extent of its own territory.

Because of spraying, most stud cats are kept in their own houses and runs. These should be as large as possible to allow for sufficient exercise. If possible, the cat should also be allowed a daily run in the garden, under supervision. It will invariably spray in each corner, marking afresh what it considers to be its own special territory.

Both neutered males and females may begin to spray after some upset, such as a move or a new kitten in the house. This may also be a way of marking the territory. Some cats, if neutered at a later age, still spray and also smell. Even if neutered, a male will frequently go through the motions of mating a calling queen, should there be one on hand. Of course, no kittens result. Two neuters may also try to mate each other, but this happens infrequently.

Owners of queens should remember that if she has been away to stud she should be kept apart from all males for ten days or more afterwards, as even if she has 'taken' (that is, even if a successful mating has occurred and she is in kitten), it is still possible for her to be mated by one or more other males. A queen may even have kittens in the same litter by two males. In other words, a dual mating will have taken place. If the official mating has been unsuccessful and the queen is let out, she may well be mated by a mongrel tom and have kittens by him. So if you value the pedigree of your kittens, keep the mated queen away from all males for at least ten days after the mating has taken place. The mechanism in the female cat during oestrus is such that the act of copulation stimulates ovulation, which means that the ova are shed at the same time as the spermatazoa enter the female. However, conception will only take place at a second mating if it occurs very soon after the first. A female will often continue accepting other male cats all through pregnancy, but any ova which have not been fertilized at the first matings will have already died.

A mature cat likes to go out and explore, and may disappear for days on end then reappear. Inset, top: a female cat 'calling'; inset, bottom: a male 'spraying' to mark territory

Cat breeding

MANY a cat lover has the ide of buying a pedigree kitten and becoming a breeder, but has little knowledge of what is involved. In the first place the kitten, whether male or female, should be chosen with breeding in mind, not bought first before breeding is decided on, although with luck this may be successful. If bought purely as a pet it is quite possible that the kitten may have bad faults, such as a kink in the tail or small eyes, which in no way detract from its desirability or attractiveness, but which nevertheless are faults which could be passed on to the progeny, preventing them from becoming prize-winners if exhibited.

If the intention is to begin breeding seriously, it is advisable to take time over the choice of a kitten. The best way is to visit one or two cat shows and to pay particular attention to the prize-winners and their appearance. Breeders should be consulted and, if possible, arrangements made to visit them and to see the kittens in their home surroundings. It is far better to be frank with a breeder and to say that you want the cat for breeding rather than to buy a kitten which is being sold for a lower price as a pet and to be disappointed with the litter she eventually produces. If at some future time these kittens were shown, they would be a bad advertisement for the mother's breeder. Cat shows are the shop windows of the cat world and a winning exhibit is always good publicity, hence the importance of telling the breeder whether the kitten is to be a pet or is intended for breeding and showing.

A novice should buy the best female kitten he can afford, as close to the recognized standard as possible, and—most important—with a good pedigree. If choosing the variety with exhibiting in mind, it is as well to remember that in the most popular varieties, such as the Siamese, the competition is strong, whereas in some other varieties—for example, the longhaired Brown Tabbies or in the Shorthairs and the Russian Blues—the numbers exhibited are smaller and the chance of producing winners is therefore greater.

As males and females usually reach the adult stage at different ages, it is not feasible to buy a breeding pair and expect kittens to arrive to order. In any case, a male cat needs more than one female to keep it happy and its owner will have to decide whether to keep at least five or six females or to advertise the male at public stud. So for the beginner it is better to buy a female kitten, sending her away to stud when she is sufficiently mature. The majority of female cats live quite happily in the house as pets, whereas with a male it will prove practically impossible to allow it the freedom of the home due to his habit of spraying. A few never spray, although this is most unusual, but some are able to live in the house without inconvenience during the winter when the females are no longer 'calling'.

A male will need a sturdy weatherproofed double-lined stud house of ample proportions, with room for a female cat who is visiting him to have a separate run inside. There should also be adequate space to allow the owner to sit inside to supervise the matings. The pen for the female should be half-boarded in to allow her some privacy, and the other half of the front covered with wire netting so that the male may talk to her and they may get to know each other before actually meeting. Some matings can take quite a time, so the owner will need somewhere to sit to take charge of the proceedings. A shelf should always be provided for the male to jump on, as some females turn on the male after mating has occurred.

Stud work requires time and a great deal of patience and it is certainly not a quick way to make money, as some queens (as breeding females are called) can be very difficult.

In addition to the house, the stud (the male cat) must have a large run with plenty of room for it to take exercise. There should be thick branches and shelves for it to jump and climb on and the whole run must be wired in at the top and made completely escape-proof.

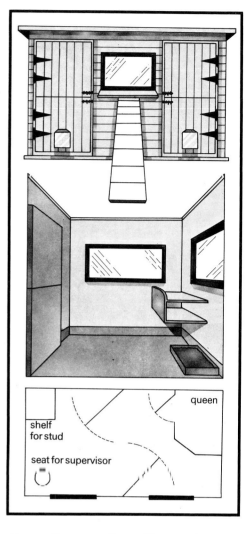

Above: diagrams of a stud house. This must be weather-proof and with room for the visiting females to have a separate run inside it.

Below: the mating about to take place. Some matings can take some time to accomplish and should always be supervised by the stud owner

If a male cat becomes a champion at shows and has already sired good stock, he will be in constant demand as a stud

A cat-door at the bottom of the house will allow it to come in and out as it wishes but this should be closed when there is a female with it. Toilet trays will have to be provided and changed regularly.

If possible, a stud should be allowed to walk around the garden each day under supervision but it is inadvisable to allow it complete freedom, particularly if at public stud. Not only may it not be around when required but it may also pick up some infection on its travels which it could pass on to visiting females. Studs are most affectionate, love their owners, and should always be given as much attention as possible.

If the male is a good one and wins at the shows, ending up by becoming a champion, and proves to produce good stock, its services will be much in demand.

The stud should not be overworked, and while young should only be allowed to mate one or two females. Its first mating should always be with an older and experienced queen.

Breeding catteries with large numbers of cats have never proved very successful, as cats greatly appreciate human companionship and affection and dislike being kept under zoo-like conditions.

It is a worthwhile and entertaining hobby to have a female pedigree cat and to allow her to have one or two litters a year but not more than two. It should be stressed that there is very little profit involved when one takes into consideration the stud fees, the cost of transport, the feeding of the kittens for nine or ten weeks, the inoculations needed against feline infectious enteritis, and the cost of brushes, combs, talcum powder, vitamins, blankets and so on.

Before a female cat is sent to stud, a booking for the male will have to be made well in advance. The Governing Council of the Cat Fancy publishes from time to time a list of cats at stud and, once a choice has been made, the premises should be visited to see the conditions under which the male is living. Everything should be spotlessly clean. The male should look lively and healthy, and its house and pen, where the female will stay, should be in good order. The stud should be looked at to ensure that it has not the same faults as any the female may have, and its pedigree should be seen to make sure that it is not too close to that of the female.

If it is impossible to have the female in the owner's house, she will have to have a house of her own in the garden. This should be similar to that described for the male, with a large run. Nevertheless, if it can be arranged, it is much easier if the female has her kittens in the owner's house. Not only will she be close at hand and can be given attention immediately if required, but the kittens will become used to humans and to being handled at an early age and so will be much more friendly and less nervous than those reared in runs.

A female may start 'calling' (come into season ready for mating) when only about six months old but this varies from breed to breed. She should never be mated at this early age, the best time being when she is about ten to eleven months old, as by then she should be fully grown and well developed. She should not, in any case, be sent to a stud at the first 'call', the second or third being preferable.

As soon as she comes into season and starts rolling around, the stud owner should be informed and arrangements made for her to be sent or taken on the second day. If possible she should be taken by the owner rather than sent by train. She will probably stay at the stud for three or four days; it is usual to allow the male to mate her twice. In the event of her not having kittens, the stud owner may agree to have her back for a further mating, free of charge except for the cost of the food, but this is not compulsory. The stud fee is payable in advance. The period of gestation for a cat is approximately 63 to 65 days but it does vary by a day or two. The female should not be allowed out for at least a week after she has been mated, as a dual conception is possible and she may meet a mongrel male in the garden and have mongrel and pedigree kittens in the same litter.

The female should be provided with a good varied diet on her return from stud. She should be restrained from tree-climbing during the last week, as the additional weight may cause her to lose her balance. A week or two before she is expected to give birth, a low box should be placed in a dark corner where the kittens may be born without interference. The box should have plenty of clean newspaper in the bottom. After the kittens' arrival the paper may be removed and replaced with a thick blanket. Most cats have their kittens with no trouble at all but, if after an hour or more the cat is still straining and no kittens have appeared, it is as well to ask the veterinary surgeon (who should have been warned in advance) to call and see all is well.

If you eventually wish to become known as a breeder, it is advisable to have a registered prefix, which is a distinguishing name used before the personal name given to a kitten. The prefix will be granted by the Governing Council of the Cat Fancy on payment of a small fee, and it will be reserved to you for life, and only allowed to be used for kittens of your breeding. Should kittens bearing your prefix do well at the shows, any others you wish to sell will be much in demand.

Preparing for the birth of kittens

A female cat, normally described as a queen, should not be mated before she is ten or eleven months old, and not until she has 'called' for a second time. In the Cat Fancy the term 'calling' is used to denote the period when a queen is in season or 'on heat', and thus ready for mating. Even if the first call does not occur before eleven months, it is still safer to wait for the second call, as frequently the first will be somewhat erratic, and she may be in season one day and not the next. During the female's first call she must, in any event, be watched to make sure that she does not slip out, to be mated by any tom-cat waiting hopefully around. Female cats differ greatly in the length of time between one call and the next, but possibly it may be every three to four weeks from early spring to autumn.

If she is a pedigree cat, a booking will have to be made some time beforehand with the owner of a suitable stud. The premises where the stud is kept should be inspected first to see that both the stud and the accommodation are in first-class condition. The queen, if a maiden, should be sent to the stud on the second day of her second call. Arrangements should be made in advance to take her by car or, failing this, to send her by train to be collected upon arrival. Before this happens, the owner should see that the queen is in the best possible condition, for this is important if she is to have a strong and healthy litter and be able to feed her offspring successfully. The queen should be having a good mixed diet, but should not be overfed, since this will make her too fat and so create difficulties when she is having the kittens. She should have been wormed according to the dosage prescribed by a veterinary surgeon. Her fur must be free of fleas, and her ears clean, with no sign of canker. Daily grooming is a 'must', to ensure there are no loose hairs in the coat, which otherwise could be licked down into the stomach and cause a fur-ball there. In particular, a long-haired cat should be on a regular weekly dose of corn or paraffin oil to make sure that this does not happen. While still a kitten she should have been inoculated against feline infectious enteritis, as a stud owner will probably not accept any female cat that has not received this treatment. FIE is highly infectious and has a high death rate.

Her stay with the stud will last for about three days, and during this time she should have had at least two matings. On her return she must be kept in for at least a week, as she may still be in season and a dual mating is always possible. Then too, the mating with the stud may not have been successful, and the queen may then have kittens by a mongrel, should she happen to meet one. A female cat must be allowed to live a normal life during pregnancy and not be pampered or treated as an invalid. For several weeks it will be difficult to know whether her visit to the stud has been successful and that she really is in kitten. The first sign may be about 21 days after the mating when the nipples may start to deepen in colour, taking on a decidedly rosy hue and also slightly increasing in size. A week or two after this, her sides may begin to develop a rounded appearance. Veterinary yeast tablets and a few drops of a vitamin oil may be given daily.

The period of gestation tends to vary by a day or two, but is usually taken to be about 65 days. The female should be allowed as much exercise as possible. But if she is a tree climber curtail this activity during the last few weeks, as, not being accustomed to the weight of the kittens, she may misjudge her capabilities and have a nasty fall. At this stage, four small meals a day are preferable to two large ones, and a milky feed may also be given if the queen is able to tolerate milk. It is essential that there should always be clean water available for her to drink.

Towards the end of the pregnancy, hard brushing of the female must be avoided, although she should have some grooming. Care should be taken that she does not strike out with her claws when her sides are touched. If she is a long-haired variety, it will be easier and cleaner for her kittens if the fur around her nipples is clipped fairly short. Whatever the variety, the nipples should be washed free of any encrustations and dirt, and softened with a little vaseline. Some breeders clip the fur short under the tail if there is no objection by the cat, but if she becomes distressed by such attention it is far better to leave it. Too much handling should be avoided, and children should certainly not be allowed to pick up or carry the female around, as unwittingly they may squeeze or even drop her and in so doing severely damage the kittens.

Cats usually give birth easily, but it is wise to be nearby in case help is needed

About two weeks before the kittens are due, the female should be introduced to a kittening box. This is advisable as some cats have their own ideas about where they are going to have their litters, perhaps showing a preference for the best bed in the house. A strong cardboard box, big enough to allow the cat to stretch out, but not so large as to risk the kittens straying too far from her and becoming cold, is suitable, as it can be burned after use. A tea chest also makes a good kittening box. The box chosen should be placed on its side, with the front partially covered in to a point high enough to stop the kittens from rolling out but not so high that the mother cannot see into it. For if she cannot look over the edge she may run the risk of jumping onto her little family. The box should be put in a quiet corner where there will be as little disturbance as possible; it should be well away from strong light, an ideal spot being the bottom of the airing cupboard. The kittens will be born blind, the eyes not opening until the tenth or eleventh day, and therefore they should not be exposed to a bright light or strong sunshine until the eyes are fully opened. A warm, even temperature is also essential for at least the first few days. Plenty of newspaper should be placed in the bottom of the box and the female shown where it is. Although the cat will not necessarily sleep in it, she will probably spend much time tearing the newspapers up into pieces, making what she considers a comfortable

bed for her future family. The paper may have to be replaced several times before the actual birth. Put a blanket in after the kittens have all been born.

It should be remembered that some cats refuse to have their kittens unless their owners are by their side, and if left on their own will refuse to stay in the box. For this reason all drawers and cupboards should be kept well closed, as these might be preferred to the box provided.

It may be difficult for a novice breeder to know when the birth is imminent. Usually, a few days before the kittens arrive, the cat begins to wander restlessly around from room to room, and this may be taken as a warning sign. If she has complete freedom, it is wise to keep an eye on her for the last day or two in case she strays from home to have her kittens in some secret hiding place.

When it becomes clear from her restlessness and the signs of movement in her flanks that the queen is about to have kittens, it is very important that the owner keeps calm and does not fuss around the cat unduly. Most cats, even maiden queens, have their kittens quite normally, doing everything that is necessary themselves without any assistance. The owner should be near at hand to give reassurance if needed, but should never attempt to interfere unless difficulties arise. Incidentally, kittens are often born during the night, so the owner should be prepared for this. Whenever the event occurs, however, certain items should be kept close at hand. Have ready some cotton wool, a mild non-toxic disinfectant, a small clean towel, a hot water bottle and a pair

of sterilized scissors – in case it is necessary to cut the umbilical cord connecting the kitten to the afterbirth (known as the placenta). An hour or two before the kittens are born, the cat's figure may change slightly in appearance, as the kittens drop in preparation for the birth.

Once the contractions have started, the queen will probably settle down quite happily in the kittening box, often purring loudly, stopping only as the contractions occur. At first, these usually take place every half-hour, the intervals between becoming shorter and shorter until the contractions may occur almost once a minute. It is impossible to predict how long the kittening will take, as this depends on the number of the kittens and their size. If possible, the queen should be left to produce the kittens without help, but should she strain for an hour or two without anything happening, and appear to be distressed, the veterinary surgeon should be informed immediately. For a novice, it is a good idea to be in touch with the vet beforehand in case his services are required.

Although reference has been made to pedigree cats, the procedure is much the same if the cat is a much loved mongrel. She will still need exactly the same care and attention, and if she should give birth to unwanted kittens (because the owner has neglected to have her spayed) she should be allowed to keep at least one. It is very cruel to take away the whole litter. Not only will the cat be most unhappy, she may also develop a breast abscess due to the milk not being taken and she will soon start calling again.

The birth of kittens

THE earlier article dealing with preparations for the birth of kittens concluded with the commencement of the contractions. After the contractions speed up, the amniotic sac–the skin bag enclosing the kitten–may be seen protruding slightly from the vagina, looking rather like a dark bubble. The queen will start licking herself, eventually breaking the sac, and helping the wet, bedraggled kitten to emerge into the world, followed by the placenta, or afterbirth.

The mother will lick the kitten all over as soon as it is born and while it is still attached to the placenta. She will start with the face, clearing the nose and mouth of any fluid, and thus encouraging the kitten to breathe. Should she fail to do this, leaving the kitten with the sac still over its face, the owner must break the sac very quickly with thumb and forefinger. The face should be wiped gently with a rough towel until the kitten opens its mouth and tries to mew. Should it appear lifeless, a gentle breathing into the mouth, similar to the kiss of life, may well revive it.

The kitten will be attached to the placenta by the umbilical cord, and the queen bites through this with her teeth, leaving between 2 to 3 inches still attached to the kitten. This remnant will eventually dry up and fall off. If the queen makes

Kittens will continue to suckle until they are three to four weeks old

no attempt to do this the owner may break the cord with thumb and forefinger, taking care not to pull, as this may cause a hernia. Alternatively, it can be cut through with a pair of sterilized scissors. About 3 inches of the cord should be left, and the broken end should be dabbed with a little mild non-toxic disinfectant.

The queen usually eats the placenta; this is said to encourage the flow of milk. If, however, a number of kittens arrive in quick succession, the queen may leave some of the placentas, and these should be thrown away. Keep count of them; there should be one placenta for each kitten. If any are left inside they may lead to infection and fever. The vet should be told immediately if this happens, as he will be able to give the queen an injection to help the uterus eject the undischarged placenta.

It is a good idea to have a small cardboard box on hand, containing a thick

blanket with a hot water bottle wrapped in it. If the kittens arrive quickly one after the other, they can be put in this box while the mother is busy with the later arrivals. Some kittens squeak very loudly if taken away, upsetting the mother, and if this happens the covered hot water bottle should be put in the end of her box, instead of removing the kittens altogether. Even though they are only a few minutes old, the kittens will struggle around by instinct to the mother's nipples, sometimes competing for the same nipple, and start to suckle.

Not all litters are born quickly. There may be half an hour or even an hour between births, in which case the cat may appreciate a drink of warm milk with

added glucose between each birth. Some cats, however, refuse to eat or drink until all the kittens have arrived.

When kittening is over, the queen, after washing all the kittens, will lick herself thoroughly and settle down for a sleep beside her family. If the movement does not disturb her, the blood-stained newspapers can be gently drawn away, and replaced by clean ones.

Later, a thick blanket should be placed in the box. It must be one that does not ruck easily, because of the risk of covering and suffocating a tiny kitten. Clean water should be put near the box for the mother to drink. For the first day only a light meal, such as fish and rabbit, should be given, as this is easily digested.

The queen's milk may not appear immediately, but the suckling by the kittens should help to bring it through.

Kittens are normally born head first, although occasionally there is a birth in which the feet appear instead—a so-called breech presentation. In this situation the queen usually manages to expel the kitten alone, although it is more difficult than the normal birth. Should straining be prolonged, it may help to induce the cat to walk around the room a little. The owner, too, may be able to assist by inserting well-greased fingers into the vagina and easing the kitten out, or by giving a gentle pull to coincide with a contraction, taking great care not to injure the kitten. In cases of extreme difficulty call the vet.

When kittening is very difficult and the births are unduly prolonged, the vet may find it necessary to perform a Caesarean operation. This will have to be done in the surgery for it requires an anaesthetic and suturing. The kittens will probably be born alive, but will have to be hand-fed for the first few days until the queen has recovered and is able to feed them herself.

Hand-feeding should be every two hours, using Lactol, or a tinned milk such as Carnation, with added boiled water and glucose. This preparation is given with a doll's feeding bottle or a dropper. One breeder has found that an artist's small paint brush dipped into the milk and then into the kitten's mouth is a very successful feeding method.

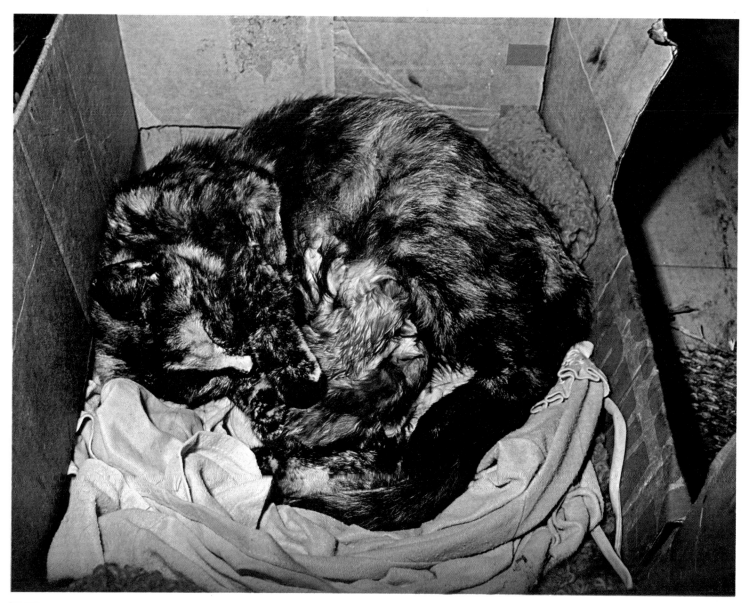

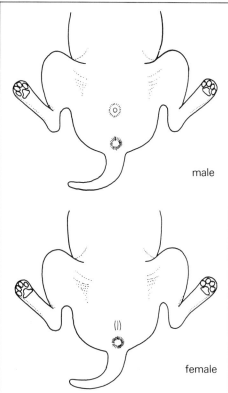

If the mother cat does not feel like washing her family for a day or two after the operation, the owner will have to do this, wiping them gently all over with a rough towel. While this is being done, the kittens should urinate and possibly excrete, as would happen when washed by the mother's tongue. As a rule, however, recovery will be rapid and even before the stitches are removed, the mother will happily be looking after and feeding her kittens.

It should be stressed that the majority of cats do have their kittens quite naturally, even purring as each one arrives. Some are so pleased with their family that at first they refuse to leave them, and it may be difficult to persuade the mother to come out of her box even to eat.

As the kittens are born blind, their box should be kept out of strong light until the eyes are fully open. This happens after about twelve days.

Although there may be a few squeaks at first, the kittens should soon settle down happily and may safely be left to the tender care of their mother. For the

Above: the queen licks a kitten as soon as it is born; others born earlier are already suckling. Left: this diagram will help when sexing kittens

next three weeks she will do all that is required in the way of washing and feeding, and if mother and offspring appear quiet and peaceful the chances are that all is well. It is important not to handle the kittens at first as this may disturb the queen and make her uneasy.

If it is important for the owner to know the sex of the kittens, and the mother has no objection to her family being handled, identification is best done an hour or two after birth, before the fur begins to grow too long, particularly in the case of Longhairs. If the kitten is a male, there will be about half an inch between the small, circular anus and the rudimentary testicles; if female, the entrance to the vagina will be seen as a small slit very close to the anus. If both sexes are present in the litter and they can be compared side by side, this will make the task of identification much simpler.

Should your cat be neutered?

IN Britain the RSPCA has estimated that there are at least a million unwanted and homeless cats and kittens destroyed each year, and in America the figure must be considerably higher. This huge number becomes understandable when we consider that a cat usually has from five to eight kittens in a litter, and can conceive again within weeks of giving birth, and that the female kitten is capable of breeding when she is between five and eight months of age. In other words, the reproductive ability of the cat is very great; it has been estimated that a litter of kittens could multiply to over a hundred within the course of a year.

What can we do about the number of unwanted cats? The only answer is to prevent cats from breeding too much by neutering as many as possible. There are also other factors that make the neutering of cats advisable. The un-neutered female, if not allowed to breed, becomes noisy, frustrated and spiteful when 'in season' and ready for mating. The un-neutered male also has his problems. His natural instinct is to look for, and fight for, a mate. He will adopt an area of garden or ground as his own and will defend it against all male cat intruders. His natural instinct is to try to increase the area of his territory. He will fight for this right and may become injured in the process.

To show which area he holds he urinates on trees, bushes, fences and walls to 'stake his claim'—an effective method as his urine has an extremely strong smell. It is an unfortunate fact that many males believe that their territory includes the house in which they live, and spray urine in the home, on curtains, chairs and even walls. Once the resultant smell is in a building it is extremely difficult to eliminate. A neutered male, if doctored before it is sexually mature, will not develop the spraying habit.

The only practical method of neutering is the surgical removal of some of the sex organs. Methods using tablets or injections are unreliable, and can have undesirable side effects. The operation of 'tying off the tubes' (vasectomy in the male, ligation of the fallopian tubes in the female) is possible but is less popular, since although the cat is rendered sterile, its sexual motivation, behaviour and instincts are not altered.

No one has ever suggested that all cats should be sterilized as, if this were done, the species would soon become extinct. The problem is rather that of which cats should be allowed to breed. As a general guide it must be said that an owner should only allow his or her cat to have a litter if it is certain that a good home can be found for *all* the kittens. It is of no benefit to a female cat to have a litter of kittens before she is spayed—as neutering of the female is commonly called. In fact, it is generally considered better to carry out the operation before the reproductive ability has developed.

The pedigree cat kept as a pet is in the same position as any other pet. There is no reason to allow her to have kittens just because she has a pedigree. As far as the male cat is concerned it is generally accepted that all kept solely as pets should be neutered. Only pedigree male cats needed for breeding should be left entire.

The male cat is neutered by castration which involves the removal of the testes. This is done under an anaesthetic so the cat feels no pain. Many years ago it was believed that a kitten under six months of age felt no pain, and so the operation was carried out without an anaesthetic if the cat was young. Because of this old and wrong idea, some people still believe that a cat can only be castrated before it has reached the age of six months.

There was some debate in the past regarding the ideal time to neuter a male cat, the conflict of opinion being influenced by the belief that a very immature cat suffers surgical bruising during the operation, that if a cat is under a certain age when neutered it might be more susceptible to bladder stones at a later date, and that an adult cat when neutered may not lose its instinctive spraying habit and may still wander and fight.

It is now generally accepted that it is best to neuter a male cat when it is between four and five months of age. By doing this the risk of surgical bruising is minimized, and the adult male characteristics have not developed. The risk of bladder trouble is considered very small, and indeed many experts consider that it is not increased by the operation.

Although there has been some argument about the ideal age for this operation, there is no dispute regarding the need for some cats to be neutered. Even an elderly cat becomes more home-loving and tends to fight less after the operation.

It is usual to withhold food and water for 12 hours before the operation. The actual operation is of short duration and the after-effects are slight. There are usually no sutures (stiches) and no need for a post-operative examination. If a cat has been trained to use a dirt-box it is sensible to keep this spotlessly clean for several days to reduce the risk of infection.

The female cat is neutered by the surgical removal, under an anaesthetic, of the uterus and ovaries. This is a more complex operation than the neutering of the male. An incision is made either at the side, or in the middle, of the abdomen. This incision is relatively small and is closed with sutures that have to be

The reproductive systems of the cat. The male cat is neutered by the removal of the testes (top). The female is neutered by the removal of the uterus and ovaries (bottom). Both operations are performed under a general anaesthetic.

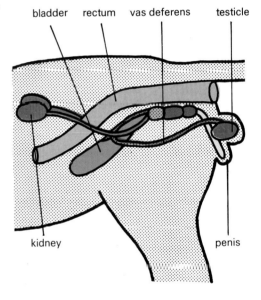

bladder   rectum   vas deferens   testicle

kidney   penis

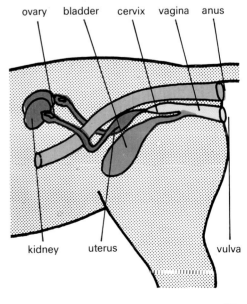

ovary   bladder   cervix   vagina   anus

kidney   uterus   vulva

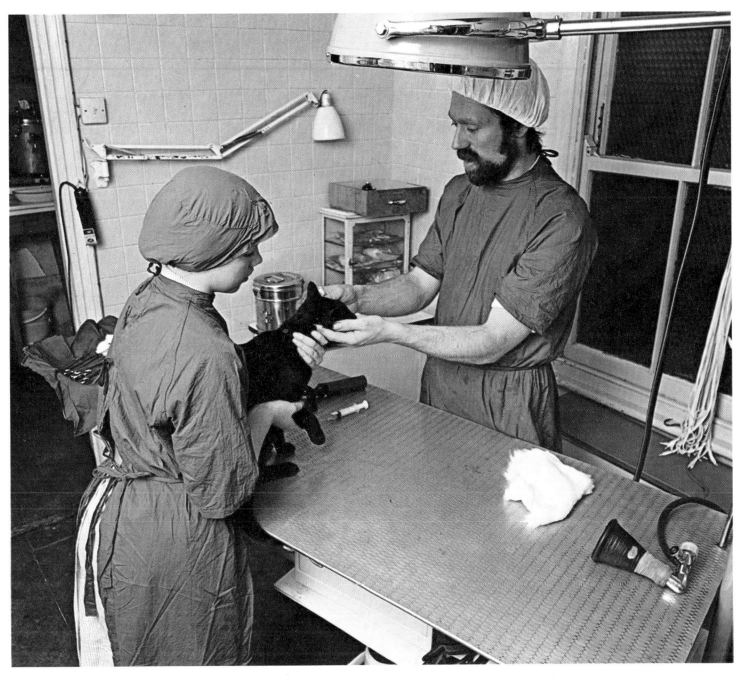

Here a cat has been brought to the veterinary surgery and is being prepared for its operation by the vet and the nurse. Left: a healthy neutered cat

removed from seven to ten days after the operation. There is a method of neutering the female cat without using sutures. This is known as the Stab Method.

It is not easy to see that the operation on the male has been carried out, but in the female an area of skin is shaved and the incision is easily seen. The operation on the female cat can be carried out at any age, but it is generally avoided if a kitten is under the age of three and a half months, if the female is heavily pregnant, or if she has just had a litter of kittens. Depending on the method used, she will be ready to return home either on the day of the operation or the following morning. It is often possible to arrange for her to be

hospitalized for a few days after the operation, but this is seldom necessary as she will recover remarkably quickly and will normally be as usual within 24 hours. It is sensible, however, to ensure that young children do not lift or play with her for a few days. If this cannot easily be prevented it is wise to arrange for the cat to stay for a short period in hospital.

The neutering of cats is a routine operation that is almost entirely without risk and should not cause worry to the owner or cat. The operation must, of course, be carried out by a veterinary surgeon. A neutered animal requires less food than the 'entire' cat. A kitten that has been neutered presents little or no problem as the owner adjusts the amount fed to the growth of the cat and so compensates for the change caused by the operation. But the owner of an adult cat that has been doctored is faced with the problem that the

cat will wish to eat as much as it did before the operation—although it should, in fact, be fed slightly less. Unless the food intake is reduced there is a danger that the cat will gradually become fat and flabby. So, with the adult cat, care over the diet for the first month after the operation will ensure health and a prolonged life.

Anyone who has brought a kitten into the household has to face this question of whether or not the new pet should be neutered. Often, however, the decision to neuter the animal is put off or avoided altogether in many instances. Yet, if you wish to consider yourself a conscientious cat owner, you must face up to the necessity for neutering unless you propose to breed cats. Some of the reasons for neutering were given at the beginning of this article. If you still feel unconvinced, make an appointment to see your vet and talk it over with him and he will advise you.

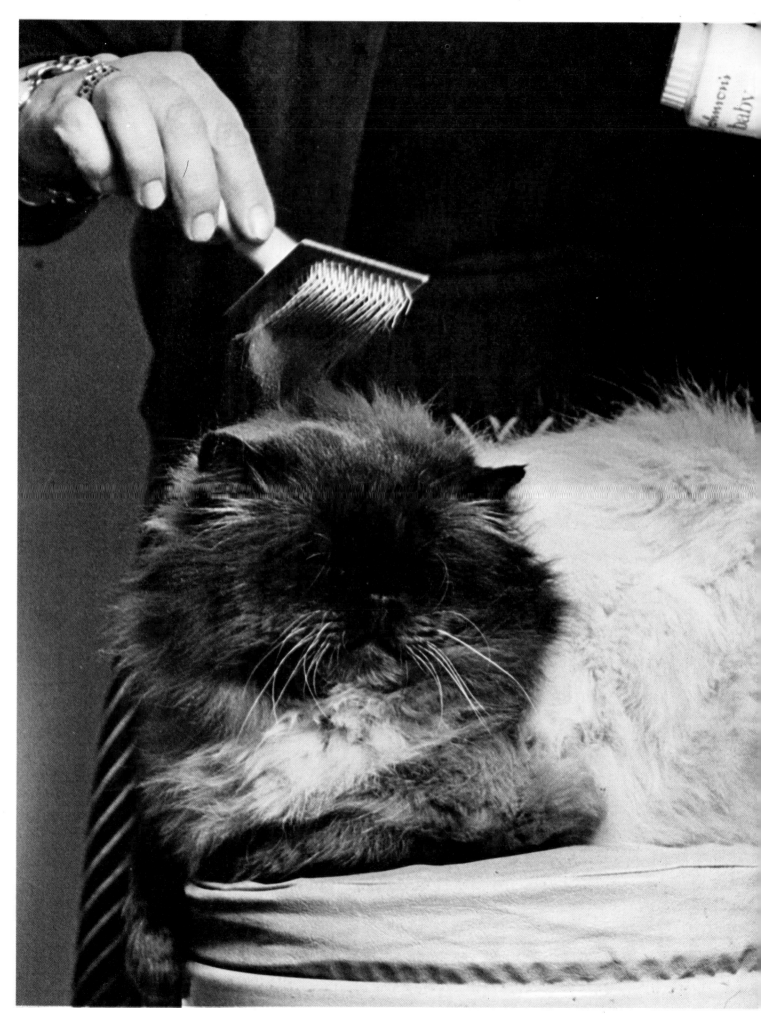

Preparing your cat for the show

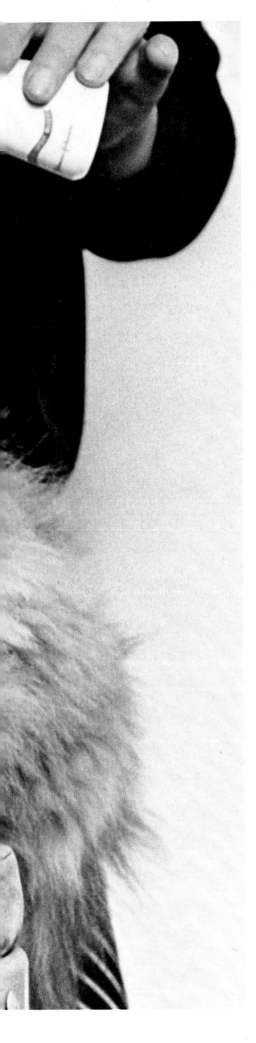

OWNERS of pedigree cats are often shy of exhibiting, feeling that because their pets do not come close enough to the particular Standard required it would be a waste of time to show them. Obviously the nearer a cat conforms to the Standard, the better its chances, but other factors, including condition, are also taken into account when awarding prizes.

The Standards are the characteristics required for the more than fifty varieties of cat currently recognized. Generally speaking, the Longhairs should have broad, round heads with neat ears and big round eyes, cobby bodies on sturdy legs, and short, full tails. The British Shorthairs should have round heads with full cheeks, shortish noses, small rounded ears, large round eyes, sturdy bodies and shortish tails. The Foreign Shorthairs, including Siamese, Burmese, Abyssinians and Russians, are required to have long, slim bodies, wedge-shaped heads with large ears, and long, tapering tails. Naturally, Standards differ slightly according to variety, apart from the colour and pattern of the coat.

If in doubt as to the wisdom of showing, remember that the perfect cat has yet to be born and that there is more than one prize-winner in every show. Little can be done if the cat on exhibit falls short of the Standard in bone structure or type, but the owner can present the cat in such a way that it looks its best and can ensure that it is in good condition. This alone may make all the difference between a first and a second prize.

Good condition does not come about by chance alone, and good presentation means more than just grooming intensively for a couple of days before the show. Ideally, show preparation begins in kittenhood, with correct feeding, daily grooming and adequate exercise. Correct feeding means a good mixed diet, but not too much food. Daily grooming is essential, not only because it gets a kitten accustomed to being handled, but also because it encourages the fur to grow in the correct manner. It is particularly im-

Talcum powder must be brushed out thoroughly when grooming a cat

portant for Longhairs, with the fur being brushed up around the head to form a frame for the face. Longhairs with pale, self-coloured coats should have talcum powder sprinkled well down into the roots of the hair, then brushed and combed out completely. Any mats in the coat should be gently teased out with the fingers or with a knitting needle. If the tangles are very bad, they may have to be cut out with round-ended scissors, but this can count against a cat that is to be shown.

Exhibitors of Whites and Chinchillas sometimes bathe their cats a few days before a show, allowing time for some of the natural grease to return, and then grooming in the normal way. If a Longhaired or Shorthaired Black is to be exhibited, it is advisable to keep it well away from damp and from strong sunlight, both of which are likely to turn the fur a brownish shade.

Grooming the Shorthairs is comparatively simple, as a gentle brushing with a soft brush will remove dirt and dust. This should be followed by a slight combing, not too much, otherwise tracks may be left in the fur, spoiling the appearance. The coat should be finished with a hard hand-stroking, which gives a wonderful gloss and is also muscle-toning. Polishing with a chamois leather is also useful for producing an extra sheen.

The ears of all varieties should be inspected daily to make sure that they are quite clean, with no suspicion of ear mites, commonly referred to as canker. It is also essential to prevent the coat harbouring fleas, the presence of which may be revealed by minute, shining specks of flea dirt. Before being admitted to the show hall, each cat is examined by a veterinary surgeon. Even if there is no sign of illness, a cat with fleas or dirty ears will certainly be refused entry, and entry fees will not be refunded as it is up to the exhibitor to ensure his cat is in good condition.

Any cat to be exhibited should be used to being handled, for one that is nervous or terrified of strangers will never show itself to best advantage. A cat may well be gentle and friendly at home, yet behave quite differently in the show hall. If it is so frightened as to bite and scratch when picked up by the steward and judge, it should not be shown again. For this and other reasons, it is better for a novice to start at a small show, such as an Exemption show, rather than at a large Championship show. Such an occasion provides an opportunity to observe details of show routine (the pace not being too frantic nor the crowds too large) and to assess a cat's reactions. The cat can also be compared with other exhibits, providing some idea of its potentialities.

Would-be exhibitors should apply to the appropriate show manager for a schedule and entry form at least eight weeks before the date of the show. A pedigree cat must be registered with the Governing Council of the Cat Fancy before it may be shown. If not bred by the exhibitor, the cat must have been transferred to him several weeks before the show.

The entry form should be filled in with the cat's name and other particulars (as given on the registration or transfer form), with the numbers of the chosen classes written in clearly. This should be returned to the show manager well before the closing date, especially as, due to the popularity of certain shows and limited accommodation in the halls, entries frequently have to be restricted. Any errors on the form may mean disqualification, so careful checking is essential before posting. If an acknowledgement is required, a self-addressed postcard should be enclosed.

A week or more before the show, the exhibitor is sent a numbered tally and vetting-in card. The number of the tally is the same as the one on the pen which the cat will occupy. The vetting-in card has to be handed to the vet when the medical examination takes place. A cat must be taken to the hall in an adequate container, such as a basket, a box or one of the sturdy cardboard cartons especially made for cats and sold by several of the Animal Welfare Societies and some pet shops. An exhibit may not be carried into the hall in the owner's arms or taken in on a lead under any circumstances.

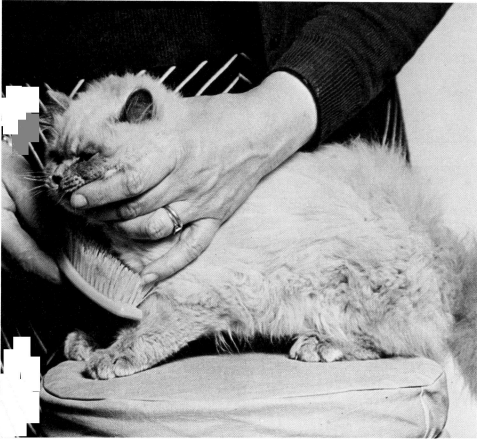

Preparing for the cat show should start the first day you take your kitten home. Diet and exercise are just as important as daily grooming. If one is to produce a winner your cat must be in peak condition

A cat that is in kitten or is still nursing a litter may not be shown, and although there is currently no definite ruling, it is unwise to exhibit a female cat that is calling. Not only may she roll all over the pen, spoiling her appearance, but the very fact that she is there may upset any full males in the vicinity, making them exceedingly difficult to handle and causing chaos throughout the show hall.

The night before the show, everything should be made ready. An early start will be necessary as there are often long queues waiting for the vet, and all cats must be in their pens ready for the judging, which starts at approximately 10 o'clock. A clean white blanket with no markings of any kind, is essential, but an open lacy type should be avoided as the cat may catch its claws in it and be difficult to disentangle from it when the steward tries to lift the cat out of the pen. A white litter tray will also be necessary, and this should not be so large as to leave too little room for the cat. Peat moss for this is provided in the hall, but some exhibitors prefer to take one of the proprietory litters or torn-up newspapers with them, as many cats seem to prefer to sleep in the litter tray rather than on their blanket. What is more, peat does tend to cling to the fur, particularly if long, ruining the appearance. Some exhibitors take cotton wool and a non-toxic diluted disinfectant to wipe out the pen as a precaution before putting their cats in.

Food is not provided by the management and some of the cat's favourite food should be prepared. Small, plain white feeding dishes should therefore be taken for this purpose and also for holding drinking water or milk. The cat should be made as comfortable as possible.

Once through the vetting, the exhibitor is allowed to go to the pen in the hall bearing the same number as on the tally. The pen will be standing on tables covered with white paper, and the bars and back should be wiped all over with the cotton wool, slightly dampened with the disinfectant. The blanket should be placed on the white paper, leaving room for the litter tray, which should be suitably filled in the manner required. Should the weather be very cold, a hot water bottle may be put under the blanket for the cat's comfort. It is not permitted to decorate the pens or give them any distinguishing marks. The food and dishes should not be put in the pen until lunchtime, when the open classes will have been judged.

Powdering is not permitted in the hall and any powder left in the fur may mean disqualification. Most exhibitors, particularly those with Longhaired cats, do the last powdering the night before, leaving some in the coat to be brushed out in the morning before entering the show.

When the pen is ready, the cat should be taken out of the basket and given a last quick grooming. The tally, already on white tape, should be tied around the neck, not too loosely in case the cat pulls it off with its claws, or too tightly so that it causes discomfort. The number of the tally will appear in the judge's book under the appropriate classes. If entering two exhibits, make sure that the correct tally is around each cat and that they are in their right pens. Such mistakes have sometimes led to cats being incorrectly judged and, of course, disqualified.

The hall is usually cleared during the morning (except at the annual National Cat Club Show at Olympia) but exhibitors are allowed to watch from the sides of the hall or from the gallery. After lunch, the public are admitted, although, quite possibly, judging of the side classes will go on all day. The owner must not approach the judge while his cat is being examined, but if there is time may ask for an opinion at the end of the day. Once the hall is cleared and catalogues are on sale, it is as well to buy one and to check that the cat is entered in the correct classes. Should there be an error, it should be pointed out at the award table.

In Britain the judge goes to the show pen accompanied by her steward carrying a small table, towel and disinfectant. There are no professional handlers for cats, as there are in the dog world, but the stewards act in a similar capacity, lifting the cats out of the pen for the judge's inspection and replacing them afterwards. A quiet, efficient steward who holds the cats correctly, not roughly but firmly to make sure they do not escape, is a great asset to a judge. Correct handling helps make a cat feel less nervous and may well lead to a prize, but a cat that cannot be handled will be passed over by the judge.

The judge will examine the cat, viewing it from all angles, mentally awarding points for the various characteristics in accordance with the recognized Standard. She will also note the way it is presented, its condition, that its eyes are bright and shining, and that it appears well nourished. Once she has made up her mind, the results are marked in her book. Slips from this book are put on the award board, and the prize cards are attached to the winning pens, according to this list.

Even if a cat is not a prize-winner at its first show, the owner will gain useful experience and a clear appreciation of what is required by the judges.

The ultimate reward comes at the end of the show when your cat is a winner and a prize card is attached to its pen. Even if unsuccessful you will gain useful experience

Cat clubs and shows

TO the general public all cat shows would seem to be very much the same and to a large extent they are. The cats are vetted in and put in cages by their owners, and are judged more or less on similar standards. The main difference between shows is in the actual method of judging.

In North America, as the judges do not go to the cages, the exhibitors are allowed to hang gaily coloured curtains inside and to put in cushions or rugs for the cats to sit on, and they may also display any ribbons and rosettes previously won. The owners may sit beside their cats and when called, take them to the judging ring and

Above: proud winners with their rosettes.
Left: a view of the National Cat Club Show

place them in the cages behind the judge who sits at a table. The judge then takes the cat from the cage and places it on his table for a complete examination.

In Britain, however, the judges go to the pens and a steward takes out the cat from its pen for the judge's examination. The owner is not permitted to go near his exhibit or to handle it. Nothing is allowed in the pen except a white blanket and a litter tray.

One or two shows in Europe adopt this procedure too, but the majority are run on similar lines to those in the USA, except that the judging may be held behind screens or in a separate room. Curtains and decorations such as rosettes and ribbons are permitted, and the owner may sit beside his exhibit. A steward goes to the pen and takes the cat to the judge. There are pens placed behind the judge's table, should the judge wish to make comparisons between certain cats. Shows in Europe, which usually last two days, can be truly international and may include exhibits from Austria, Belgium, Holland, Germany, France, Switzerland, Italy and Scandinavia. Shows under the jurisdiction of the Federation Internationale Feline d'Europe, usually referred to as F.I.F.E., and a number of independent cat associations, are held in a number of countries in Europe, including those already mentioned. The Scandinavian countries and Czechoslovakia all hold their own shows.

Australia, New Zealand, Rhodesia and South Africa all organize a number of shows each year, and cats are judged in a similar way and to similar standards as those in British shows.

There are more than 50 cat clubs scattered all over the British Isles, and the majority of them are affiliated to the Governing Council of the Cat Fancy. This is the registering body and serves the same function for cats as the Kennel Club does for pedigree dogs. Shows held under the Council's auspices abide by its rules and regulations.

In North America and Canada there are nine registering bodies, all of which have independent cat clubs affiliated to them. They include the Cat Fanciers Association, (this alone looks after the interests of nearly 380 clubs), the Canadian Cat Association, the American Cat Association, the American Cat Fanciers Association, the Cat Fanciers Federation, the Crown Cat Fanciers Association, the National Cat Fanciers Association, and the United Federation. The standards recognized by each of these different associations are much the same, which makes it easy for judges to preside over any of the shows which the different bodies might organize. Cats can be shown in either the United States or Canada without any difficulty and judges can officiate in either country.

The individual clubs either cater for members interested in any or all varieties of cats or they are specialist clubs catering for a particular variety or varieties, such as the Blue Persian Cat Society and the Burmese Cat Club.

Novices are recommended to join the club nearest them, perhaps joining others later. The advantages of belonging to a club is that one meets fanciers with similar interests. If intending to exhibit, a member may enter the classes guaranteed by that club at various shows and compete for the special prizes offered. Should the club be responsible for organizing the show, members pay reduced fees for entering the classes, which can be a great saving. In addition, the club will probably be offering cups, rosettes and other prizes for members only.

In Britain, three types of show are held: Championship, Sanction and Exemption. At a Championship show, challenge certificates are awarded to the adult winners of the open breed classes, provided they are up to standard. When the cat has had three such wins under three different judges at three shows, it can claim the title of Champion. Sanction shows are rehearsals for Championship shows in that the rules and regulations are the same, but no challenge certificates are given. Exemption shows are much smaller, their rules are not so stringent, and they are ideal for novices starting to exhibit. They enable novices to learn show procedure, to meet and talk to judges and to see how their cats fare in competition.

The largest cat show held anywhere in the world is the National Cat Club's show, usually held at Olympia in London, in late November or early December. It attracts an entry of about 2,000 cats and kittens, which includes both pedigree and pet cats. The other shows vary considerably in size, from an Exemption show with perhaps 100 exhibits, to the larger Championship shows with entries of 700 to 800. The Kensington Cat Club show is unique, as only kittens and neuters are exhibited. This is usually held in London in late July. There are other equally important shows held in Scotland and Wales and, indeed, throughout Britain. A full list of these may be obtained from the Secretary of the Governing Council of the Cat Fancy.

One of the largest shows in North America is held every March in Madison Square Gardens in New York. Most of the shows in the USA and Canada are really three or four shows in one. The organizing club is responsible for the All-Breed Show (which must be entered by all cats), another club is responsible for the Longhair Speciality show, a third for the Shorthair Speciality show and possibly a fourth on All-Breeds. A cat may be entered in three of these shows and, if outstanding, can be judged the Best Cat in all of them. Four judges officiate.

The classes are much the same throughout the cat world, with the exception of Britain which has many more; clubs put on their own classes at the shows of other clubs. Apart from the open class, the choice of other classes varies, ranging from 'breeders' to 'novice'.

The classes are divided into colour or variety and into male and female classes. There is a Novice class for cats which have never won a prize as an adult, an Open class for those which have a recorded win, a class for those already champions, and a Grand Champion class, the result of which is decided on a points basis and takes into consideration the number of champions beaten. There are also classes for International Champions and International Grand Champions; the cats in these have to be a champion or grand champion in more than one country. Such a title would be impossible in Britain where the quarantine regulations preclude a cat from leaving the country to attend other shows. There are also kitten classes for those between the age of four and eight months. Neuters have similar classes to those for entire adult cats, but do not compete with them.

The method of entering a show is much the same in all countries. An application for the schedule or premium sheet and entry form or entry blank should be made to the appropriate authority at least two months before the show. The schedule gives details of the rules, regulations and classes as well as the names of the judges.

When the entry form is received, it should be studied carefully. The open or breed class is the most important in Britain, as a win in this class is a good advertisement for the owner, particularly of a stud or a breeding queen, as the kittens from that strain will then be in demand. Also, of course, three wins in this class enable a cat to bear the much sought-after title of Champion. The entry form must be filled in with the details exactly as set out on the cat's registration or transfer form. The cat's name, date of birth, parentage, variety and registration number must all be entered correctly, as wrong information can lead to disqualification.

Left: the judging in progress. Judges are assisted by a steward who holds the cat

Chapter II
The Longhairs

The Birman

THE Birman long-haired cat, also referred to as the Sacred Cat of Burma, is a very striking and beautiful variety. It has the characteristic coat pattern seen in the Siamese and in the Colourpoints (Himalayans), of a pale body colouring with dark points, but it differs from the other pedigree cats in having the attraction of white paws.

Said by some to have originated in France many years ago from cross-breeding, legend has it that the Birmans are the descendants of a very old variety found in Burma centuries ago. The story goes that in the Temple of Lao-Tsun, where a golden goddess with blue eyes, Tsun-Kyan-Kse, was worshipped, the priests lived with their sacred cats. The many times told legend relates that when the temple was attacked by raiders, the head priest was killed while meditating before the goddess. By his side was his pure white cat, Sinh, his faithful companion, who put his paws on the body of his dead master, defying the enemy. As he did this, his body fur turned golden, the colour of the goddess, while his paws

Although the Birman has dark points like the Siamese, its paws are white, a symbol of purity according to legend

remained white, a symbol of purity. His legs, face, ears and tail became earth-coloured, and the yellow eyes turned a sapphire blue.

Sinh stayed in front of the goddess for seven days, refusing all food. Then he died, taking with him the perfect soul of the old priest to paradise. When the priests met to choose a successor to the head priest, the hundred white cats of the Temple, came slowly into the chamber, and to the amazement of the priests, all were no longer white, but had taken on the same colouring as that of the dead Sinh. They formed a circle around one young priest, Ligoa, who was chosen as the new head priest. The story is told in slightly differing versions but basically is much the same.

Whatever their origin, the Birmans were recognized in France as long ago as 1925, but the numbers there gradually declined and it was not until the Second World War that the variety really became known, and they appeared at a number of cat shows in Europe. The Birmans were seen in Britain in the early 1960s, and recognition was granted by the Governing Council of the Cat Fancy in 1966.

The British Standard calls for a cat with a wide round head, with full cheeks, a long low body on short strong legs, and a bushy tail. The tail is not required to be as short as in other Longhairs. The fur should be long, but is not so profuse as in other varieties; the texture is silky, and

curls slightly on the stomach. The nose is longish rather than snub; in the North American Standards it is referred to as being of Roman type.

The body fur is creamy-golden in colour, with the points (that is the mask, ears, legs and tail) being a darker colouring, The points may be Seal, a definite dark brown; Blue, a bluey-grey; Chocolate, milk chocolate; and Lilac, a lilac-grey hue. Other points colourings are possible. The eyes should be a deep blue, but vary slightly in intensity according to the points.

The most distinctive feature, the white paws, should appear as gloves on the front legs, ending in an even line along the paws, while those on the back should be gloved the same as the front paws but the white should form gauntlets on the back of the back legs, going up to a point. Ideally these gauntlets should match in size and shape, as should the gloves on the front paws, but it is difficult to breed a cat with perfect gloves. The body fur is not so luxurious as that of the majority of the long-haired cats, and for that reason the coats rarely mat, and so are easier to groom and to keep in order. A Birman is ideal for a cat lover who likes cats with long fur but has not the time needed for intensive grooming. However, it should be stressed that they still need daily grooming to keep their immaculate appearance.

Birmans, like other breeds that ori-

ginated in the Orient, are sexy cats. When the queen comes into season and is ready for mating she will certainly let you know. Far more than the queens of European breeds, she puts on quite a performance; in addition to the 'calling' there will be much rubbing against the legs of her owner and against the furniture.

She will have her first season before she is seven months old – even at five months if she is particularly precocious. But she should not be allowed to mate at that time; many undomesticated cats such as one sees on railways embankments are mothers before they have left kittenhood! A domesticated cat whose owner cares for her well-being will not allow mating to take place until at least the second call, by which time the Birman will be 9 or 10 months old. By then she should be fully grown. It may be, of course, that the owner decides not to mate his female, and if this is the case, then the queen should be neutered.

Cats are like humans: if they are frustrated they become on edge, even developing a mild mental illness such as a neurosis. Certainly a queen should be mated not later than her third season.

What the Birman owner will soon realize is that this breed is not regular in coming into season; like most Orientals there is not the consistent regularity in oestrus that one finds with the European cats. Therefore the owner has to be watchful, otherwise an unwise mating may occur.

The kittens are born almost white with the contrasting points appearing in a few weeks. As all kittens have blue eyes, it is difficult to appreciate for some weeks how deep the colouring will eventually become. Gay and lively, they are soon clambering out of their box and rushing madly around, quickly learning to use their sanitary trays.

Friendly, intelligent cats, Birmans show affection readily. Quiet in voice, they make ideal companions. Perhaps because of their slightly longer bodies, in general they kitten easily, the average litter being about four or five in number. They make good mothers.

As already stated, Birmans are comparatively easy to groom, because of their fur texture. They are also very clean cats and usually keep themselves looking spotless. Powder can be used on the pale body fur, but care must be taken that it is brushed out completely, particularly if the cat is to be shown, as any left in the dark points would appear as white specks looking like scurf. A soft, pure-bristle brush should be used and a fairly narrow toothed steel comb, to avoid leaving track marks in the fur.

If the cat is being exhibited and its white paws appear to be at all dirty or stained,

they can be washed carefully by putting each paw in turn in a shallow bowl with a little warm water. Baby shampoo should be rubbed in and then well rinsed out, the paws being dried completely. It is as well to keep the cat indoors until it is time to leave for the show.

There is no similarity between the Birman and the Burmese, the latter being a short haired cat of foreign type. Although the coat pattern and the eye colour of Colourpoints and Birmans are very much alike, it is not advisable to mate the two varieties together. It may well lead to the introduction of white toes into the Colourpoints and/or loss of the gloves and wrong type into the Birmans.

To all owners of a Birman, the words of Theophile Gautier, the famous French writer of the early nineteenth century, will find an instant response. Gautier was a great cat lover, and to the surprise of many visitors to his home he preferred talking about cats rather than literature. In one of his most memorable passages about cats he had this to say – and it applies particularly, I think, to the Birman:

'To gain the friendship of a cat is a difficult thing. The cat is a philosophical, methodical, quiet animal, tenacious of its

Unlike most Longhairs, the Birman does not have a snub nose. Its long, silky fur does not mat easily, and is simple to groom

own habits, fond of order and cleanliness, and it does not lightly confer its friendship. If you are worthy of its affection, a cat will be your friend but never your slave. He keeps his free will, though he loves, and he will not do for you what he thinks unreasonable; but, if he once gives himself to you it is with absolute confidence and affection! He makes himself the companion of your hours of solitude, melancholy and toil. He remains for whole evenings on your knee, uttering his contented purr, happy to be with you, and forsaking the company of animals of his own species. In vain do melodious mewings on the roof invite him to one of those cat parties in which fish bones play the part of tea and cakes; he is not to be tempted away from you. Put him down and he will jump up again, with a sort of cooing sound that is like a gentle reproach; and sometimes he will sit upon the carpet in front of you, looking at you with eyes so melting, so caressing, and so human, that they almost frighten you; for it is impossible to believe that a soul is not there.'

Two-colour Longhair cats

THE term 'two-colour' as applied to longhaired cats can mean, firstly, a breed where the colours intermingle, and secondly, a breed where the colours are in distinct patches. The first type of two-colour Longhair cat to be considered is the Blue Cream. These are unusual Longhairs in that they are genetically sex-linked, so that they are invariably females. Males have appeared occasionally, but tend to be sterile. There is no evidence that they have sired kittens or even that they were true Blue Creams.

The British Standard calls for a cat with a good broad head, with tiny well-placed ears, a short broad nose and big round copper or orange eyes. The body should be cobby on short thick legs and the tail short and flowing. The dense silky coat should be in pastel shades of blue and cream; the two colours are to be softly intermingled, giving the impression of shot silk. It is difficult to produce such a coat to perfection, but in America, where the type and other characteristics required are much the same, there is one vital difference in that the coat should be well broken into bright and well-defined patches. These seem to be easier to produce, but are considered a fault in Britain.

In both countries a cream blaze on the face is liked.

Blue Creams were known in the comparatively early days of the Cat Fancy when, to improve the type of the early Creams (or Fawns as they were then called), various cross-matings were tried. They appeared in litters, but were looked on as oddities and were frequently referred to as Blue Tortoiseshells and were sold as pets. Gradually it was realized that by selective breeding it was possible to breed these Longhair kittens to order and, depending on the male used, Blue Creams could produce variously coloured litters.

They were first recognized in Britain in 1929 and over the years have become very popular. The mixed breeding from Longhair Blues and Creams has produced cats of a very high standard, with excellent type. A number have won the highest award of Best in Show when exhibited.

Gentle, affectionate cats, they are very companionable, making a great fuss of their owners. Good mothers, loving their kittens, a Blue Cream with her litter is most photogenic and is often to be seen in the colour pages of magazines and on chocolate boxes.

Careful grooming is required, with talcum powder being sprinkled well into the coat and then brushed and combed out completely, so that the fur stands up, giving a true shot silk effect. A soft bristle brush should be used, never a harsh one.

For those interested in the breeding of the Longhair Blue Cream, the genetics involved are similar to those for producing Tortoiseshells. In fact, Blue Creams do sometimes appear in litters from Tortoiseshells, but are usually produced by cross-breeding the Blues with the Creams. A Cream male mated to a Blue female may produce Blue Cream females and Blue males. A Blue male mated to a Cream female may produce Blue Cream females and Cream males. A Cream male mated to a Blue Cream female may produce Blue Cream females, Cream females, Cream males, and Blue males. Mated to a Blue, a Blue Cream female could have Blue Cream females, Blue males and females, and Cream males.

Cats with coats of two colours, where the colours are in distinct patches, have been known in the Cat Fancy since the early days of pedigree breeding. They

The Black and White is one of the most striking of the Longhair Bicolour cats

which was so exacting that it proved impossible to produce cats with such a pattern. Invariably judges withheld the challenge certificates which disgruntled the breeders.

In 1971, the Governing Council of the Cat Fancy in Britain agreed that the Standard should be amended. This now says that not more than two thirds of the coat should be coloured and not more than a half to be white. The face should be patched with colour and white. The fur should be long and flowing, silky in texture, and extra long on the frill and short tail. The head should be round and broad with good width between the small ears, the body cobby and massive on short sturdy legs. The big round eyes should be orange or copper in colour. Faults are tabby markings, yellow or green eyes and white hairs in the coloured sections.

Any solid colour is permitted with the white, and some very good examples have been seen at the shows, with probably the Black and Whites being the most striking. Very pretty Red and Whites, Blue and Whites and Cream and Whites have also been exhibited and there are now a number of Champions.

They are large cats, and make strong, healthy pets or good breeding stock. The females kitten easily, usually producing multi-coloured litters, but all most attractive. Feeding the Bicolour is no problem

The Longhair Bicolour appears in several colours; any solid colour with white is permitted in the Standard. Above: the Red and White, and right: the Blue and White are both very pretty cats with their long, silky fur and round eyes

were seen in shows in the Any Other Colour classes and were listed as Blue and White, Orange and White, Tabby and White, and Black and White, the latter being known as Magpies. These were the forerunners of what are today known as Bicolours. Although apparently much admired and with the kittens selling readily, from the breeders' point of view they were of little interest, and the numbers became fewer and fewer.

Around 1960, a breeder in Britain realized that, produced from selected breeding stock, a correctly bred Longhair Bicolour could be used in the breeding of Tortoiseshell-and-Whites. Until then, they more or less appeared by chance in litters. It is essential that any Bicolour male to be used as a stud with the idea of producing such kittens should have been bred from a Tortoiseshell-and-White queen.

To aid the breeding programme, the Longhair Bicolours were granted recognition in 1966 and an approved Standard was set out. This was based on the pattern of markings as for the Dutch rabbit,

as it is not a fussy eater, doing well on a varied diet. These Longhairs keep themselves very clean, but daily grooming is essential. Powder could be carefully sprinkled into the white patches should they look dingy, but great care must be taken to avoid any getting into the coloured sections, as this would give them a dull appearance.

In common with all the Longhairs, the two-colour varieties are likely to develop hairballs, or furballs as they are sometimes called, unless stringent precautions are taken. The cat's habit of licking its fur is responsible in part for this condition developing, although Nature has also provided the cat with an instinct to chew grass which acts as an emetic. The grass brings on regurgitation, during the course of which the hairball is expelled through the mouth. It also acts on the bowels and causes the hairball–if in the intestines–to be evacuated. This natural defence against the serious effects of hairballs operated well enough thousands of years ago when the cat was not so domesticated as it is today. Nowadays, however, many cats in towns have no access to grass, so their owners have to aid the expulsion of hair balls by artificial means.

A dose of vegetable oil–corn or olive– given once a week will assist in the natural process of getting rid of the hairball. The oil can either be given on a spoon, or placed in a saucer from which the cat will lick down a dose by itself–it has an instinct that tells it that the oil is necessary, just as it knows when grass is necessary. Some breeders who live in towns, away from natural sources of grass, will grow grass in pots specially for their pets. This is a good plan and should be followed wherever possible.

Longhairs are more likely to suffer from this complaint than Shorthairs, simply because of the length of the coat, but it is a constant danger to all cats, and in particular to those whose owners do not take the trouble to groom their pets as regularly as possible.

When grooming is neglected, a very great quantity of fur will be swallowed by Longhairs in the course of the licking which goes on several times daily. This hair forms in the intestines into a sausage-like shape with the consistency of matting. If it is not got rid of by natural means, a surgical operation will certainly be necessary. So it is in the owner's interest– and essential to his cat's well-being–to see that such a situation does not arise. Surgical operations can be costly affairs and, of course, unpleasant for the cat, though not fatal.

In the early stages of the obstruction, the signs will be mild constipation, and later vomiting. Finally, a complete stoppage will result. Hairballs can be felt in

the stomach or intestines, but it is advisable for the owner to get his diagnosis verified by a veterinary surgeon if he suspects their presence. In some instances an X-ray may be necessary to confirm the condition. The vet may try to get rid of the hairballs by giving your cat a laxative –olive oil or liquid paraffin–but in severe cases an operation may be the only way of saving the cat's life.

A pleasant way to prevent the condition from getting to the extreme stage described is to include tinned sardines in your cat's diet. If this seems expensive, the sardines can be eaten by the owner, and the oil and bits of fish left in the tin given to the cat, first making sure that there are no sharp edges likely to cut the cat's mouth.

However, all this can be avoided if the owner will give ten minutes a day to grooming his pet. So many cat owners act on the assumption that because a cat is not pedigree or–if it is–will not be exhibited at cat shows, then no grooming is necessary. All domestic cats need grooming by their owners. Not only does it help prevent the formation of hairballs, because the hair you remove by grooming is not there to be licked into the cat's stomach, but it makes your cat look so much more presentable. The natural beauty of a cat is brought out by daily

The Longhair Blue Cream differs from the Bicolour in the shading of its coat, which is pastel blue and cream merging together

grooming as well as ensuring the coat remains in peak condition.

Generally, two combs are advisable for the Longhairs, one with fine or close teeth that removes fleas and dust, and one with wide teeth for general grooming. Most breeders prefer bristle brushes rather than the plastic or wire variety.

The cat should be given a good brushing and combing, followed by special attention to the hair around shoulders and head to create a frill around the face. All matted hair must, of course, be teased out–but if you give the cat the grooming treatment daily there is not likely to be much, if any, matting.

The routine of grooming should be started when the pet is just a kitten. If you have just acquired the kitten, leave it for a few days to settle into the new surroundings before grooming it. Even the Longhair kitten will have a short coat at this stage, but the grooming routine is more important at this stage than the effect of the grooming itself. It will become part of its life and, in general, something to be looked forward to, for the cat is being given concentrated attention–and all cats love this.

The Cameo Longhair

THE Cameos are frequently referred to as a modern variety, but they were in fact being bred as long ago as 1954. Many years prior to this, 'pink' male kittens had appeared in litters from Tortoiseshell and Smoke matings at the Vanaki Cattery in Wisconsin. These kittens were so attractive that a planned breeding programme was started. This involved various cross-breedings using Silvers, Smokes, Reds, Creams and Tortoiseshells and one Cameo resulted from a Blue-Cream being mated to a white male whose father was a Smoke.

Dr Rachael Salisbury was very successful at breeding the Cameo and produced many beautiful specimens. A little later Barbara Naviaux also produced good specimens of this breed. It was not an easy variety to produce to order and many years were to elapse before the perfect Cameos, such as those seen at today's cat shows, appeared.

A number of colour variations are possible and Cameos can be bred with cream or red tippings, but red seems to be most favoured at the moment. The intensity of the tipping varies from one part of the cat's body to another.

In America all the Longhairs (or Persians) have one basic standard for the general characteristics required, that is that the head should be broad, the nose short, snubbed, and with a stop, the cheeks full, the jaws powerful, the ears small and rounded and the eyes large and round. The body should be cobby on low, thick, strong legs and the tail should be short and full. The fur should be long all over the body, with a full ruff round the neck, which, although of a fine texture, should be long and thick. When a colour or coat pattern of a Longhair is established and given recognition, the type required is as for other Longhairs. There are four basic Cameos: the Shell Cameo, the Shaded Cameo, the Red or Smoke Cameo and the Cameo Tabby. The Shell Cameo is sometimes referred to as the Red Chinchilla, a name which gives a very good idea of its appearance.

Cameos have been bred in the USA since 1954. There are comparatively few bred in Britain at the present time, but their numbers are gradually increasing. There are four basic types of Cameos, all of which are very attractive like this shaded variety shown here

It should have a white undercoat, with fur on the back, flanks, head and tail delicately tipped with red, with very slight shaded tippings on the face and legs. The chin, ear tufts, stomach and chest should be white. The rims of the brilliant copper eyes should be rose-coloured as should the paw pads and nose leather.

The Shaded Cameo should have a white undercoat and the tippings should take the form of shadings giving the appearance of a red mantle. The intensity of the shadings varies from deep red on the sides, face and tail to ivory white on the underside; the eyes and other colourings should be the same as the Shell.

Another attractive colouring is seen in the Red or Smoke Cameo. The Smoke from the distance may look like a red cat, and it is only in motion that the white contrasting undercoat is seen. The points and mask should be red, but when the fur there is parted, white may be seen close to the skin. The eye colour, rims and paw pads are as for the other Cameos. Tabby markings and brown tinges are looked upon as faults.

Cameo Tabbies are also recognized, but as yet they are not quite so popular as the other three variations. The under colour should be off-white with red markings, the eyes and other colourings as for all Cameos. It is also possible to produce a Cameo Tortoiseshell with a silver-white undercoat and tortoiseshell tippings.

Cross-breeding has resulted in Cameos with excellent Longhair type and outstanding eye colour. It has been suggested that a Chinchilla would make a good outcross, but that would mean the introduction of sea-green eye colouring which is exceedingly difficult to breed out.

At birth it is difficult to be sure that a certain kitten in a litter is a Cameo, as it will probably be almost white, but after a few weeks, the tippings and amount of colouring are soon apparent.

Whatever the variation, the Cameo seems to have universal appeal, always attracting attention at the show. They seem very aware of their striking appearance and accept the admiration of the public as their right.

As well as in the United States and Canada, Cameos are being bred in Australia, New Zealand, South Africa and Europe. Comparatively few have been seen in Britain to date, but now the numbers there are gradually increasing.

Longhair Colourpoints

THE Colourpoints are a striking example of a carefully planned, man-made variety. First recognized in Britain in 1955, their distinctive appearance, with a coat pattern differing completely from that of other longhaired cats, soon made them very popular. Although they have the typical Siamese colouring (that is, a pale body with dark or contrasting mask, legs and tail), the fur is long and silky, and the type that of the Longhairs.

The head is broad and round, with neat ears tilted forward; the nose is short and broad, and the large, round eyes are blue. Cobby in build, with short, sturdy legs and a short, full tail, the modern Colourpoint has already been awarded many prizes at shows, even winning the coveted honour of Best in Show.

A number of fanciers in the past had often considered the possibilities of breeding such a cat, but since they had little

knowledge then of the genetics involved, they gave it up as a bad job. In fact, as long ago as 1922, a cross-mating between a White Longhair and a Siamese was attempted in Sweden, but nothing more was done. In the United States, prior to World War Two, Mrs V. Cobb and Dr Clyde Keller mated several Siamese to differently coloured Longhairs, and eventually succeeded in producing a longhaired Siamese. Unfortunately, the war inter-

Of the longhaired cat breeds, the Colour-point seems to need the least grooming of all to keep its fur in an immaculate condition

vened and the experiments were stopped. Over the years chance matings produced cats with the correct coat pattern, some-times with Longhair type.

It was in 1947, in Britain, that the late Brian Stirling-Webb saw such a cat. Having a profound knowledge of genetics, he became interested in producing a pedigree variety with good longhaired features and Siamese colouration. He worked for many years on this, using the best Blue and Black Longhairs of the time, eventually producing the Colourpoint. This was a cat with good type, full coat and, most difficult of all, large blue eyes.

By a strange coincidence, in the United States at the same time, a Mrs Goforth was carrying out a similar breeding pro-gramme, not realizing that Mr Stirling-Webb was doing the same in Britain. She too succeeded in breeding such cats, but they became known as Himalayans, in view of the fact that their coat pattern resembled that of the rabbits of this name. These were granted recognition in 1957, and are increasing in popularity.

Both countries nowadays produce out-standing cats with good type and various points colouring, including Seal, Blue, Chocolate, Lilac, Tortie, Red and Cream. Colourpoints can be mated to Colour-points, but some fanciers still use the occasional outcross to an outstanding self-

trial breedings, with many kittens having to be neutered and given away as pets, before specimens as good as those now seen on the show bench will be produced. It is therefore far better to purchase the best Colourpoint female kitten that can be afforded and start from there.

The Governing Council of the Cat Fancy has laid down standards for the Colourpoint and these must be strictly adhered to if winners are to be produced. It states that the fur should be long, thick and soft in texture, with a full frill round the neck. The colour should be Seal, Blue or Chocolate-pointed with appropriate body colour as for Siamese (that is, cream, glacial white or ivory respectively). Points should be densely coloured, and if there is any body shading it should be the same colour as the points.

The head should be broad and round and wide between the ears; the face and nose should be short, with small, tufted ears and well-developed cheeks. Eyes should be large, round and full and a clear bright blue, the deeper the blue the better.

The Colourpoint should have a cobby body and be low on the leg. The tail is short and full and not tapering.

Colourpoints were recognized by the Governing Council of the Cat Fancy in 1955. Above: a beautiful Chocolate Point. Right: a Blue Point kitten

coloured Longhair, hoping to ensure that there is no loss of type in the resultant kittens. When mating Colourpoint to Colourpoint, it is important that only male and females of the best type should be used. The main problem is to keep and intensify the colouring of the blue eyes.

Faults which would be penalized by judges are any similarity to Siamese (apart from the coat pattern and eye colouring), kinks in the tails, white hairs in the dark points, and squints.

Like those of the Siamese, the kittens are almost white when born, with the points colouration appearing as the fur grows. They are delightful, with their fluffy coats and big blue eyes, and are usually very self-reliant. They should be kept warm when young, but otherwise need no special attention, growing into fine, healthy cats.

Each Colourpoint is an individualist, but generally their temperaments are equable and their intelligence high. Playful and gay, but quiet by nature, they appear to have inherited many of the good points of both the Siamese and the Longhair. They are less noisy in voice than many Siamese, give their affection generously and love companionship.

Anyone interested in breeding Colourpoints should remember that although Longhaired Siamese can be produced comparatively easily, it takes many years of

Longhair Tabbies

IN the dictionary the word 'tabby' is defined as 'a brindled or streaked cat; a material made of a watered fabric; to give a wavy or watered appearance (to material) by pressure between hot rollers.' The word is said to have been derived from Attibiya, a district in Baghdad where watered silk was made many centuries ago, and as the cats' markings resembled that of the material, they too were referred to as tabby.

The original long-coated cats seen in Europe were said to have come from Ankara (then Angora) in Turkey and from Persia, and to have had self-coloured fur, that is, the same colour all over. Writers in the early days of the Cat Fancy in Britain spoke of cats from Russia which had dark brown fur with some tabby markings. It is probable that these inter-mated with the original Longhairs, as did the resident domestic shorthairs, and so the tabbies with long fur originated. It is a fact that there are more cats with tabby markings than any other but few have the exact pattern desired (since it varies from one side of the cat to the other), and those that have are usually short-coated.

There are three colour variations recognized in Britain, all requiring the same striking pattern of markings. These are the Browns, the Silvers and the Reds, while in America there are also the Blues, the Creams and the Cameos, but all should have the same tabby markings.

These markings must be clear cut, standing out distinctly from the background colour. On the forehead the markings should resemble a letter M and the lines around the eyes should have the appearance of spectacles. There should be swirls on the cheeks and delicate pencillings on the face. Unbroken rings should encircle the neck – these are referred to as the 'Lord Mayor's chains'.

There should be a wide dorsal stripe running along the whole length of the body to the ringed tail, and, on the flanks and saddle, deep bands of a contrasting or deeper colour than the main background colouring. Looking down on the shoulders the pattern should resemble a large butterfly, made up of circles, stripes and blotches. Around the legs should be 'bracelets' and even the stomach should bear some markings. The markings are less obvious than in the Shorthair, being obscured by the long fur.

The type is as for most other Longhairs, the heads being broad and round, with small ears, short broad noses and full cheeks. The bodies should be cobby on short, strong legs, the tails short and full, and the fur long and flowing.

It is difficult to get a very good type in the Brown and Silver Tabbies, although this has been achieved in some Reds. The main trouble is finding suitable matings. Mating Brown to Brown for many generations invariably means loss of type and of the rich brown sable colour. Many matings have been tried in order to breed out the upright ears and long noses which sometimes occur and to improve the

tabby markings. The Silver Tabbies are improving and some very good specimens have been shown recently.

At the early cat shows, there were a number of outstanding Brown Tabbies, but as fanciers realized the difficulty of reproducing the exacting pattern, less and less were bred.

When first born the kittens are very dark, showing little of the well-defined markings, but these appear as the fur grows and it is not easy to tell for the first few months which one is likely to be a future champion. The ground colour should be a warm sable brown, with the markings jet black, while the eyes may be hazel or copper in colour. Bad faults are white chins, white tips to tails, and brind-

Markings of Longhair Tabbies must be clear-cut, as on these Longhair Red Tabbies (opposite page and left) and the Longhair Silver Tabby kitten (below)

ling (that is different coloured hairs in the black markings or in the brown coat), and such cats should not be used for breeding.

The Silver Tabbies are delightful cats, most striking in appearance with their silver fur and dense black markings. Many were seen at the early cat shows but few would have been classed as good specimens by today's standards. Many had bluish coats, rather than silver, possibly due to cross-matings with Blue Persians, and the markings were far from distinct. The markings should be clear and not smudged or brindled. Brown tinges in the fur are a bad fault. The type of the early Silvers was poor and frequently the ears were big and the noses long. Various crosses were tried and the coat colour greatly improved over the years. Frequently, shaded Silvers (cats with silver coats and dark shadings rather

than markings) were produced from these cross-matings and also produced, it is believed, the first Chinchillas. At first both the latter variety and the Silver Tabbies were all recognized and given separate classes at the shows but eventually, because of the difficulty in distinguishing between light Shaded Silvers and dark Chinchillas, the Shaded Silvers were no longer recognized in Britain. They are still recognized in America, parts of Europe, Australia and some other countries.

In Britain at the beginning of the century, the Silver Tabbies were still the centre of arguments, with some fanciers preferring cats with orange eyes, and others green. The British standard says that the eyes may be green or hazel. It is said that the numbers of Silver Tabbies dropped considerably in the days when breeders first started to breed for green eyes. More recently the numbers have increased at the shows, some having very good type, including one or two outstanding champions. The kittens are born dark, with little gleams of silver, but after a month or two the pale silver coats and contrasting markings begin to appear. Silver Tabbies may be mated to Silver Tabbies but in an

The markings on the forehead of Longhair Tabbies should resemble an M. There should be 'spectacles' around the eyes

effort to improve the type if not good enough, a Black or Blue stud may be used, although this may result in some loss of eye colour. Faults are brown tinges in the fur, blurred markings and brindling.

Grooming is important and should be started at an early age to encourage the fur to grow so that it stands away from the body. Talcum powder may be used, sprinkled down into the roots and then brushed completely out, working from the head back. No trace of powder must be left, otherwise it may dull the dense black markings. Although the grooming of all Longhairs is a more laborious task than the grooming of Shorthairs, if it is done regularly (every day if possible) without missing a long period when the hair has a chance to become matted, it can be done with comparatively little effort. It is also important to give the cat a general examination at the same time, paying special attention to the corners of the eyes. Any brownish matter should be wiped away with damp cotton-wool.

Red Tabbies first appeared at the shows in the same classes as the Browns, but both varieties frequently had some white in the coats and very few had the correct pattern of markings. In 1900 the newly-formed specialist club for these varieties drew up new standards and subsequently the Reds were given a class of their own. They were,

however, known as 'Orange Self or Tabby', as the colour in those days was more this colour than Red. Few, too, had markings, being mostly self-coloured and nearly all had the white chins and white tips to the tails that are still considered faults today.

Many crosses were tried, and today fanciers have succeeded in producing cats with deep, almost mahogany coats. The pattern of markings should be an even richer, darker red and should stand out quite clearly from the background coat, an effect not always easy to achieve in the long fur. The type is frequently very good, with the required short noses, broad heads and copper-coloured eyes.

Contrary to popular belief, a Red Tabby is not always a male. There are more Red Tabby males than females due to the fact that when Tortoiseshell and Tortoiseshell and White cats are mated by Red Tabbies, the red kittens in the litters will be males. However, when a pure-bred Red Tabby male mates with a pure-bred Red female, there may be both sexes in the litter.

Even when newly born, Red Tabby kittens show distinct tabby markings and it is possible then to foretell which will have the correct pattern when adult. The kittens are most distinctive, with their bright red coats. Like all the Longhair Tabbies, they are lively, very intelligent and much loved as pets.

Longhair tipped cats

NOBODY really knows how the Longhair cats known as Smokes originated. It is thought, however, that the first specimens appeared quite by chance, possibly from matings between Whites, Blacks and Blues. In any event, they have been in existence now for many years, for even at shows held towards the end of the nineteenth century, classes for this variety were well filled. One early writer spoke of seeing one at a show in Brighton, describing it as 'a beauty with black tips to the white hair, the white being scarcely visible unless the hair was parted.' This remains a good description of a Smoke.

As a result of the First World War there was a sharp decline in the numbers of pedigree cats being bred, and the Smoke was one of the worst casualties. Only in comparatively recent years has there been any significant increase. Today, thanks to several dedicated breeders, beautiful Smokes are once more being bred and exhibited at shows.

A handsome Smoke is one of the most striking of all the Longhairs. Frequently referred to as the 'cat of contrasts', it appears, at first sight, to be black, with a silver frill and ear tufts. It is not until the fur is parted that the silvery white undercoat is seen. The mask and legs should be black, but close observation will reveal a certain whiteness around the roots even in these areas. The type should be that for other Longhairs, with the eyes orange- or copper-coloured. In Britain, the Smoke is recognized in two colours: the Black and the Blue. In the latter the blue colouring replaces the black. In the United States there is also a Red Smoke, in which the white fur is tipped with deep red.

The kittens are born black or blue, depending on the breeding, and for a few weeks the novice will find it extremely difficult to decide whether they are in fact Smokes, particularly if bred from a Black or a Blue. The experienced breeder, however, is usually able to detect tiny white tippings around the eyes. It is unwise, therefore, for the novice to register the kittens too early. It has often happened

The Smoke's attraction stems from the contrast of the undercolour, which is silver tipped with black, and the dark points on the back, head and feet. Ear-tufts, flanks and frill are light coloured

that a Smoke has been registered as a Black, and a Black (because of the greyish fur of the young kitten) as a Smoke. When shown, such a kitten has sometimes been disqualified for being entered in the wrong class. By the time the adult stage is reached, there can be no possible room for error, as the contrasting coat is revealed in its full beauty.

A Smoke may be mated to a Smoke, but if this is done indefinitely, there is usually some loss of type, and tabby markings may appear. Blacks are recommended as an outcross in the case of Black Smokes, and Blues for Blue Smokes, although some breeders advocate using

Below: the Smoke type stipulates orange-or copper-coloured eyes. Facing page: the Chinchilla has a white coat tipped with black, and black-rimmed eyes

Whites. It is possible for Smokes and Blacks (or Blues) to appear in the same litter, and these self-coloured kittens would be most useful for further Smoke breeding. More recently, Chinchillas have been used, frequently with success, but as they have sea-green eyes there is always the danger that the deep copper eye colour required in the Standard for Smokes may be lost. Silver Tabbies have also been used, but with these there is a likelihood that undesirable tabby markings may be introduced. It is possible to breed Shorthair Smokes, and several have been seen in Britain. They are more common, however, in the United States, and are recognized in both countries.

Grooming is essential to keep a Smoke looking beautiful. Talcum powder may be sprinkled into the white roots but must be brushed and combed out, otherwise

the black will look greyish. The undercoat should be well brushed up, so that it gleams through the black fur. As with the Black, the coat of the Smoke is badly affected by sun and rain, soon resulting in the appearance of brown tinges; this is a serious handicap for show purposes.

The Chinchilla is one of the loveliest Longhairs, with the long, flowing white coat delicately tipped with black, giving the cat an ethereal appearance. The variety was developed as long ago as 1894, when a smoky-coloured kitten was mated to a Silver Tabby. A kitten from this litter subsequently produced a male, Silver Lambkin, said to be the first Chinchilla stud. This cat may still be seen stuffed in the Natural History Museum in London, but its colouring is dark and bears little resemblance to the champion cats of today.

The Chinchilla's coat should be pure white, with light tickings on head, ears, sides, back and tail. The ticking must never be too heavy or in patches. The eyes are unusual and extremely striking, being emerald or blue-green, rimmed with black or dark brown. The nose, too, is distinctive, with a deep brick-red tip. The type is as for the other breeds of Longhairs, but there is a tendency for the bone to be finer. Despite its fairy-like appearance, the Chinchilla is usually a sturdy,

healthy cat and has frequently been judged Best in Show. Faults in the Chinchilla are lack of ticking, over-heavy ticking, patches, poor eye colour, and yellow tinges in the fur.

The kittens are born dark, with shadow tabby markings and rings on the tail. These fade as the fur grows, and often the darkest kitten in the litter will become the most promising adult.

In the early days of cat breeding, kittens sometimes had very heavy shadings, and these were known as Shaded Silvers. Unfortunately, judges found it difficult to make a clear distinction between very dark Chinchillas and very light Shaded Silvers; consequently the Shaded Silvers are no longer recognized in Britain. In the United States, however, the Standard is now far more explicit, and both varieties are still recognized. Cross-breeding has taken place between Blues and Chinchillas, producing a variety, as yet unrecognized, referred to as the Blue Chinchilla. Blues were used as studs in the first place, when there were only one or two Chinchilla studs, but this resulted in loss of eye colour and dark-coated cats.

Very much in the public eye, partly because of their frequent appearances in television advertisements, the numbers of Chinchillas are increasing rapidly, and the kittens are very much in demand.

The Maine Coon

THE Maine Coon is one of the oldest varieties of cat known in the United States and, although no early records were kept, it is thought that they originated through cross-matings of the local cats with those that had arrived on sailing ships calling in at Maine from all over the world. Many of the latter were of exotic appearance and unusual-looking, compared with most cats in the States at that time, so much so that sailors and travellers brought them home as pets, although some probably escaped from ships and remained on land when the ships sailed. The resident cats were short-coated, descendants of those which had arrived with the early settlers, but the newcomers in many cases had long fur. Writing in an early cat book, Mr F R Pierce tells of owning, with a brother, as early as 1861, an outstanding black Maine, pointed with white, which was given the splendid name of 'Captain Jenks of the Horse Marines'. Nothing was known of its previous history. He refers to the large number of splendid Brown Tabbies with long coats to be found on the Maine coast, and also refers to a friend's blue eyed White, whose great grandfather had been brought to Rockport, Maine, from France many years before. An outstanding Maine Coon was 'Richelieu', a silver or bluish Tabby, which won several first prizes and appeared at the Limit Show of the hundred best cats at Bangor in Maine in 1884. This cat was said to be rather a 'coarse-grained variety', weighing about twenty pounds, and had apparently come from a drug store.

There are references to other kinds of Maine cats, which show that the mixed breeding had produced all colours, patterns and coat lengths. The cross-matings resulted in tough, hardy, handsome cats, and the many summer visitors who visited the Maine coast, and still do, from other parts of the States admired the unusual cats and kittens. Many were taken home to become neutered pets.

Varying colours were known, but many had fur and colouring resembling that of the racoon, and before it was realized that it was a biological impossibility, many thought that the cats were the result of crossing cats with racoons, hence the name.

Even before the first official cat show was held, the Coons had their own shows in Maine where the Maine State Champion Cat of the Year was chosen. Sadly, by 1904 the numbers had diminished to such an extent that for several decades little was heard of them. This may have been due to the fact that cat shows were being held all over the States, and the cats with known pedigrees, with longer fur and different type, were much favoured, more or less as a status symbol. Many had been imported from Britain where they were being bred by Royalty and High Society.

Much later Mrs Robert Whittmore became interested in the Coons and thought it a great pity that they were dying out, and so decided to do something about reviving the breed. She was most successful in her effort and in the early 1950s, the Central Maine Coon club was formed. The club ran shows solely for Coons and helped considerably in renewing their early popularity. In 1968 the formation of the Maine Coon Breeders and Fanciers' Association meant that the Standard was officially recognized by several Organizations and this led to an immediate increase in Coon numbers.

A striking feature of the Maine Coon is its size; it is larger than most cats, and weighs up to thirty pounds. It is a strong, sturdy animal with a silky flowing coat of soft texture, and its muscular body stands on long legs. The tail is long, bushy, and tapering at the end, with no kinks. The head is not as round as that of most other Longhairs, but rather resembles that of the early Angoras in shape and length, being of medium width with high cheek bones and a nose of medium length with little or no break. The ears are large, tallish and invariably tufted. Its most expressive eyes are large and round, the colour being green or in keeping with the coat colour. Any coat colour or pattern is allowed.

Quiet, affectionate and highly intelligent cats, they are much liked as pets, particularly as, having little or no undercoat, the fur is very easy to groom. The kittens are in steady demand, but as they usually have only one litter a year, there may be a waiting list.

The Maine Coon cat can be a variety of colours, as can be seen from the pictures shown here. This breed is unknown in Britain but has been recognized by many of the councils in the USA since 1968

Self-Coloured Longhairs

HOW and when the first long-haired cats originated no one is sure. It is known that they were first reported in Europe towards the end of the sixteenth century, having come from Angora (now Ankara) in Turkey. Others followed from Persia (now Iran). They were originally referred to as Angoras and then Persians, but the name now generally used in America and Britain is Longhairs.

The Whites and Blacks are the oldest varieties of this breed and they appeared at the first cat shows in their own classes, while the Blues were entered as 'Any Other Variety', as few of this type were without some tabby markings and white patches. It was quite some time later that the Creams and Reds were developed. These then are the five varieties of this breed now recognised by the British Governing Council of the Cat Fancy.

All should have the typical conformation of the longhair type: the heads should be broad and round, with good width between the small ears, the noses short and broad, the cheeks well developed, and the muzzles broad. The large eyes should be full and round, with no signs of green rims. The bodies should be cobby and low on sturdy legs, with large, firm and round paws, and the fur long, thick and silky in texture. The short full tails should not taper, and should have no sign of a kink.

The Blacks have never appeared at the shows in great numbers, although some splendid specimens have been exhibited. The coat should be a dense black right through to the roots, but it is not seen at

To keep the longhair White looking immaculate, regular grooming is required

frequently deaf. This element of deafness still persists in certain strains, but it would be wrong to say that all blue-eyed Whites are deaf. There are also Whites with odd eyes, that is one eye orange and one blue. Sometimes these cats can hear on the orange side, but not on the blue, although some have perfect hearing. It is also possible to have Whites with orange eyes.

At the shows the orange-eyed frequently won. In Britain in the 1930s it was decided in all fairness that there should be two classes. The Whites with orange eyes are now outstanding and have become one of the most popular varieties. The blue-eyed variety has also improved over the years, but the numbers have not increased to any extent. To help the breeders of the blue-eyed Whites, the Governing Council of the Cat Fancy in Britain has now recognized the odd-eyed Whites as they are so useful for breeding both varieties, but do not yet have Championship status as they do in America, where some outstanding specimens have been bred.

The kittens are pinkish when born, but the fur grows rapidly and in a few short weeks they are delightful, with their big blue eyes. As all kittens have blue eyes for the first few weeks of their life, it is difficult to know what the ultimate colour will be. The fur should be a pure white. Daily grooming is essential, although the Whites are not so difficult to keep looking im-

In the cat fancy five self-coloured longhairs are recognized. On this page two are shown. Left: a beautiful self-colour Cream with copper eyes. Below: a self-colour Black

its best until the cat reaches adulthood. This occurs at about nine months. Black kittens are frequently disappointing, because they have rusty-looking coats often sprinkled with white hairs, but it is a fact that the kitten with the greyest fur can grow into an outstanding champion, with a beautiful jet black coat.

The Black is one of the most difficult of the longhaired varieties to present in top show condition. The fur reacts quickly to strong sunlight and damp, and brownish streaks seem to appear almost in a day. Daily grooming is important to ensure that all the old hairs are removed. Talcum powder must not be used as it gives the fur a dull appearance; instead breeders advocate sprinkling a little eau-de-cologne well into the coat, avoiding the eyes. After rubbing dry, the fur should be brushed and combed and finally polished all over with a piece of velvet or a chamois leather. The type, which is the same as for other longhairs, is usually very good. The eyes should be a deep orange or copper colour.

The original longhairs, the Angoras, were white with blue eyes and were

type and large copper eyes. Faults are very pale undercoats, white tip to the tail, too red a coat (known as 'hot') particularly along the spine, and any bars or tabby markings.

Matings with Blues may produce Blue-Creams, Creams and Blues. Creams are also used to mate to Blacks, Tortoiseshell and Whites, and Tortoiseshells.

The Red Selfs are one of the rarest varieties of longhaired cats, owing to the difficulty of breeding cats with no tabby markings. Once they almost died out. The numbers are still relatively few, but the type of those seen at the shows is now very good, as is the deep rich red colouring of the fur. Invariably there are some tabby markings on the head and faint rings on the tail.

In America, there is also a variety known as the Peke-faced Red. This may be a Red Self or Tabby. It is not a recognized breed in Britain.

Above: any shade of blue is permitted in the self-colour Blue but it must be the same shade all over. Below right: Red Selfs are perhaps the rarest of longhairs

maculate as might be supposed. Talcum powder should be used and brushed right out. Some breeders bath their cats a few days before a show.

The Blues have always been one of the most popular of the longhairs, although they have changed a great deal from the early days of the Cat Fancy when they had tabby markings and most had some white patches. The type of many Blues is still outstanding and comes very close to the set standard. Any shade of blue is permitted, but it must be the same all over. The eyes should be deep orange or copper. Faults are green rims, white hairs in the fur, and a kink in the tail which today would mean disqualification in a show.

Blues are mated to Creams to produce the most attractive Blue-Creams, and are also used to improve the type in other varieties. They have also been used in the breeding of new varieties, such as colour-points. The kittens when first born frequently have shadow tabby markings which vanish as the fur grows. They are most attractive; quiet by nature but full of fun. Even the adults seem to be kitten-like in the way they play.

A variety which has become increasingly popular over the years is the Cream, now frequently rivalling the Blue in type. They were not one of the original long-hair colours, but apparently appeared as 'sports', a distinct variation from the normal type, in litters from Orange or Red matings. They were considered of little value and were usually sold as pets. Over the years, selective breeding has produced some outstanding Creams, with excellent

Longhair Tortoiseshells

LONG-HAIRED Tortoiseshell cats are very attractive but, because of the difficulty in breeding them, they are comparatively rare. The recognized Standard for the variety calls for an animal with a round and broad head, with small, well-placed ears, a short broad nose, and full round cheeks; the big round eyes should be a deep orange or copper in colour, while the cobby body should be on short sturdy legs. The long flowing coat should have clearly defined patches of red, black and cream. The patches should be entirely free of white hairs or tabby markings, and should also be evenly distributed all over the body, with the legs, tail and head being patched, including the tips of the ears. Black should never predominate, and the paws should not be solid in colour. A blaze in cream or red, (a solid mark running up from the nose to the forehead) is liked by the breeders, and it certainly adds character to the face. It is exceedingly difficult to get the distinct patching to show up clearly in the long fur, and correct grooming is important to make every hair stand up to allow the colour to be seen clearly.

This is one of the all-female varieties, and although males are born from time to time, they are usually sterile or are not true Tortoiseshells, having tabby markings in some form or another somewhere on the coat. It is therefore exceedingly difficult to produce Tortoiseshells to order, although they do appear in mongrel litters–but these are usually shorthaired.

This scarcity of male Tortoiseshells has, of course, encouraged some shady dealing in the past. People who were not well-informed about the breed, and who were unaware that even if a male was found it would be sterile, have been persuaded to part with large sums to acquire a stud Tortoiseshell.

In 1849, in a popular magazine, *Ladies Cabinet*, there was a report of a Tortoiseshell tom cat put up for sale at an auction. The possibility of being able to have such a breed at stud, with the likelihood of financial gains to be made, encouraged many of those present at the auction to bid for this cat. After fierce bidding the successful purchaser was an elderly lady who paid no less than £22.50 for the cat–a really high price in those days.

The cat was taken back to her home and appeared to settle down well, but after a few days a sickness overcame it. The press report called this 'a weakness of the eyes and loss of appetite.' Not unnaturally its new owner did all she could to restore this valuable tom cat to health.

On the advice of a knowledgeable friend she made preparations to give the cat a hot bath–but of milk, not of water because of the common belief that cats dislike water.

When the milk was warm enough it was poured into a basin, and the cat was gently but firmly persuaded to sit in it. To the surprise and, later, the consternation of the owner, the milk became discoloured. When the cat was lifted out it was no longer a Tortoiseshell, but a black-and-white Longhair. The red in the coat had been lost in the milk. The unsuspecting buyer had been unscrupulously cheated of her money.

All breeds of cat have their ardent supporters, and the Tortoiseshell is no exception. Of course, some individual cats possess greater 'personality' than others. One of these was owned by William Cowper, the poet who often wrote about his pet to his friends. On one occasion he called his Tortoiseshell kitten 'the drollest of all creatures that ever wore a cat's skin'. In a letter to Lady Hesketh in November 1787 he gave a description of the kitten's behaviour: 'Her gambols are not to be described, and would be incredible if they could. She tumbles head over heels several times together, she lays her cheek on the ground and presents her rump at you with an air of most supreme disdain. From this posture she rises to dance on her hind feet, an exercise she performs with all the grace imaginable, and she closes those various exhibitions with a loud smack of her lips, which for want of greater propriety of expression we call spitting. But though all cats spit, no cat ever produced such a sound as she does.'

When endeavouring to breed Tortoiseshells, breeders usually choose a stud of one of the coat colours; that is cream, black or red Self. A red tabby should be avoided, as this may mean the introduction of tabby markings, which is a fault and one, moreover, exceedingly difficult to breed out. Whatever stud is chosen, however, a Tortoiseshell's kittens are most attractive and may be of varying colours, such as cream, black, blue-cream,

The Tortoiseshell-and-White Longhair has the same black, red and cream patches as the Tortoiseshell, but with white

red and the occasional kitten like the mother. The Tortoiseshell kittens are born dark and it may be a month or two before their colour potentialities can be assessed. Tortoiseshells make excellent mothers.

Although this is an old variety, it has very little history and the early pedigrees are difficult to trace. They were appearing at the cat shows at the beginning of the twentieth century, being shown by many well-known fanciers of that period, but the numbers declined because of the difficulty in breeding. In recent years, however, interest has revived and the classes at the shows have now been quite well filled, and some outstanding specimens have been entered.

Tortoiseshells are not difficult cats to groom, but powder should not be used as this may dull the colours and, because of the difficulty in brushing out completely, may appear as white specks in the fur. The long silky fur does not seem to matt up as does that of other varieties. Only a good, soft brush should be used, and a steel comb with wide teeth. The fur should be brushed up to form a frame to the head, and special care should be taken with the tail: it is important to brush it out to its full width, so that it appears to be as nearly as wide as the body.

They are not fussy feeders, and do well on raw meat. They usually like milk, but should be always able to drink water if they wish, as should all cats.

The general standard for the Tortoise-shell-and-White (known as the Calico cat

both the Tortoiseshell and the Tortoise-shell-and-White, 50 are allowed for the coat alone.

The coat of this most attractive variety should have patches of black, red and cream, well distributed and broken, and interspersed with white. The colours should be as bright as possible, with white on the chest, underparts, feet and legs, but there should not be too much white overall, nor too little. Judges like some white on the back, and a white blaze on the face running down from the forehead to the nose is also liked.

The Tortie-and-White is another all-female variety, and until recently it was thought impossible to breed them to order, due to the lack of suitable studs. In Britain, however, one breeder was successful in doing just this, using the comparatively newly recognized Bicolours as

goes into the colour patches, as this may give them a dull appearance.

Affectionate and companionable, they usually prove to be good, loving mothers. They prefer to do everything for themselves when kittening and require little attention from their owners, although some like to have their human companions close at hand. Even when a Bicolour stud is used, not all the kittens may be like the mother; but whatever the colouring, they are most attractive, very lively and gay, playing endlessly with their mother. The demand for such kittens usually exceeds the supply.

Although known and recognized for many years and appearing at the very early shows, there is very little recorded history about them apart from the names of the cats. Many were of unknown parentage. It is apparent that the fanciers at the beginning of the century tried a number of crosses in an endeavour to produce kittens like the mothers, often with little success. It is known that they have been and still are found in litters on farms where there are a number of cats of varying colours, but these Tortie-and-Whites are invariably short-haired. It is said that from such cats the colour was introduced in the first place into the longhaired variety, but this was probably more by chance than planning.

Would-be cat owners who are anxious to acquire a Tortoiseshell or Tortie-and-White Longhair may have to wait some time before achieving this ambition. It is extremely unlikely they will be fortunate enough in their search to get one of this variety other than from a recognized breeder. The casual methods of acquiring cats that some people employ – accepting a kitten from a litter that a neighbour wishes to dispose of, visiting a home for stray cats and choosing one of the unfortunate inmates are not likely to produce the much sought-after Tortie and Tortie-and-White.

By far the best method, although it may also be the most expensive in money terms, is to go to a recognized breeder. Before doing this, it is well worthwhile to visit several cat shows and to see for yourself the type of cat you are planning to acquire. You can find out when and where the principal cat shows are being held, either by writing to the secretary of the Governing Council of the Cat Fancy, or – perhaps the easier method – by buying a copy of the fortnightly magazine *Fur and Feather* in which all cat shows are advertised and in the columns of which most reputable breeders advertise. Remember that in order to own a pedigree cat in good condition it is well worthwhile taking a little trouble in the first instance, not only for your own satisfaction but for the good of the breed as a whole.

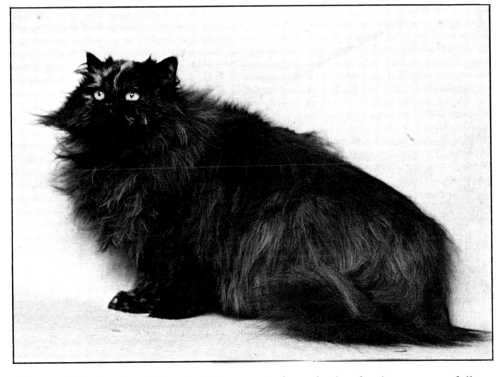

It is very difficult to breed Tortoiseshell Longhair cats, and the stud must be chosen very carefully

in North America) is as for most other Longhairs; that is, the head should be round and broad, with neat, well-placed, tufted ears. The nose should be short and broad, and the cheeks full and round. The large round eyes may be orange or copper in colour. The body should be cobby on sturdy short legs, and the coat long and flowing, being extra long on the brush and frill. The tail should be short and full, not tapering at the end, and without a kink. In the Standard for the breed 100 points are allocated for the various characteristics required, as is the case for all recognized varieties. These are distributed according to the importance placed upon these characteristics, and in the case of

studs, and other fanciers are now following her example. Black-and-White or Red-and-White males seem to be most successful, provided they come from Tortoise-shell-and-White mothers. The use of males bred from solid breeding should be avoided. The pedigree of any male to be used as a stud should therefore be carefully studied before a booking is made for a queen. Males do appear occasionally with tortoiseshell-and-white colouring but invariably prove to be sterile.

In spite of the white in their coats, most cats of this variety keep themselves looking immaculate and seldom need bathing. Their coats rarely mat, and daily brushing and combing alone will remove the loose hair and give the fur a natural shine. Powder may be used on the white parts if this is thought necessary, but extreme care must be taken to make sure that none

Turkish cats

FOR centuries the Turkish Cat has been known in the Lake Van area in south-eastern Turkey, and appears to be a natural, not a 'man-made' variety, as are so many other Longhair breeds. It was first seen in Britain in 1955, having been brought to this country by Miss Laura Lushington, a visitor to Turkey who had been intrigued by the distinctive colouring of this breed and by its liking for water. As well as playing with water, it had a reputation in its country of origin for swimming in warm pools and shallow rivers, a very unusual feat for a cat. Although it is a fallacy to say that all cats hate water, (some love to play in the sink, while others will sit out in the rain) very few take willingly to it to the extent of swimming, unless forced to do so. The Turkish Cat is therefore often referred to as the swimming cat.

The first pair of Turkish cats that came to Britain proved to breed true; that is to say they produced kittens exactly like themselves. Establishing the variety was of necessity a long task, as all cats entering Britain from overseas have to go into quarantine for a compulsory six months as a prevention against the introduction of rabies. Once out of quarantine, they had to be bred from until it was definitely proved that they always bred true, and the pedigrees showed three generations of pure breeding. So it was not until 1969, when there were sufficient people interested in Turkish cats and the numbers warranted it, that the Governing Council of the Cat Fancy approved a Standard and granted them full championship status.

The Standard calls for a cat with chalk white fur with no trace of yellow, and auburn markings on the face with a white blaze, and with the faintly ringed tail also being auburn in colour. The fur should be soft and silky to the roots. It should be long, but the coat is never so profuse as that of most other Longhair cats.

In type, the Turkish are much the same as the original Angoras, once seen frequently in Britain. These cats, which were the first long-haired cats to be imported to Britain, had longish noses, upright ears and long bodies, and at first were much in demand, but they gradually vanished with the arrival of long-haired cats from Persia. The Persians had shorter noses, smaller ears and cobbier bodies, and were preferred to the earlier arrivals.

The head of the Turkish cat should be

The beautiful and unusual Turkish cat was recognized in Britain in 1969, and is as yet unknown in the USA

short and wedge-shaped, with a longish nose. The large ears (which are set close together) should be white outside and a delicate shell pink inside, and well feathered; the nose tip and pads should be the same pink. The round eyes should be light amber in colour, and are rimmed with pink skin. The long, sturdy body should be on legs of medium length. The tail or 'brush' should be full but slightly tapering, of medium length, with the auburn rings being quite distinct in kittenhood, but faint in adult cats.

In many cases, the cats have irregular, small, auburn markings. But this does not necessarily warrant disqualification, although naturally such markings would count against a cat if it had to be judged against another as good but with no irregular markings.

Turkish cats make good mothers, kittening easily. The litters average three to four in number, and the kittens are usually well advanced for their age, running around when only three weeks old. More males are born than females.

The Turkish cats have fairly large appetites and enjoy a mixed diet, but raw meat is essential in their feeding. They are not usually very fond of milk, but enjoy drinking water.

They are easy to groom, as the fur is not so long as in most other long-haired varieties, nor do they have the woolly undercoat which makes for tangles. They should, however, have a short grooming session each day to remove the old hair and to keep them looking immaculate. Probably because of the climate of their country of origin, they tend to lose their fur during the hot weather when, in Turkey, it would be very unpleasant for them to carry a full coat. Then they may look almost short-coated.

As the weather gets colder, the coat grows very quickly. Because the fur is soft and silky, it should not be over-combed as this makes it fly up, spoiling the appearance. It is better to use a soft, rather than hard, bristle brush on the coat, with particular attention being paid to the tail, brushing it outwards to its full width.

The Turkish cats as known in Britain have not yet been bred in the USA. However, comparatively recently, cats have been introduced there direct from the Zoological Gardens in Ankara. Their type is the same as that of the Turkish cats, but they are pure white with no auburn markings. They have been recognized in the USA and are known there as the Turkish Angoras.

A few years ago, Turkey realized that people were interested in their cats and a small breeding programme is now being carried out at one of the Turkish zoos to stop them dying out, but the animals there are apparently pure white.

The Turkish Angora

THE first Longhair cats known were said to be those from Angora (now Ankara) in Turkey. They were taken to Europe by early travellers and later arrived in the United States. A writer on cats in 1868 said that 'The Cat of Angora is a beautiful variety, with silvery hair of fine silken texture . . . Some are yellowish and others olive.' Many of the Angoras first seen were white and these were the most favoured, but other colours were known.

The first cat shows created a general interest in cats, and the Angoras with their long flowing fur were much admired. However, cats with long coats then followed from Persia and were known as Persians; they became more popular than the Angoras and this eventually meant that the Angoras disappeared altogether, as the type of the Persians was much preferred then. Cross-matings were carried out indiscriminately and kittens showing Angora type were discarded as they were not considered good show stock.

It is interesting that Harrison Weir (who organized the first official cat show in Britain in 1872), when setting out the points of excellence for cat judges in his book 'Our Cats', distinguished the Angoras and the Persians by the coats alone, saying that the fur of the Persian should be fine, silky and very soft while that of the Angora was slightly woolly in texture. The colours for both were given as identical. In the main text he does say that the Angora should have a small head, large full eyes and large pointed ears, very much the description of the Turkish Angoras which have now been revived in the United States with great success. It is nice, in these days when one reads so much about vanishing species, to know of one variety which is becoming numerous again.

In 1954, a fancier imported a Turkish Angora into the USA and later others arrived direct from the Istanbul and Ankara Zoos. These were all Whites, some with blue eyes, some with amber eyes, and others with an eye of each colour. Two associations were formed in due course to look after the interests of this variety. A standard was approved and eventually the Cat Fanciers' Association gave them championship status. The Standard now accepted by the American associations calls for a cat with a small to medium-sized head, wide at the top, but tapering to a gently rounded chin; the slightly almond-shaped eyes may be amber, blue or odd-eyed; the tall ears should be wide at the base, pointed and tufted. The body should be long and graceful on high legs, with small, round, dainty paws, and the full tail should be long and tapering. The coat should be pure white, and the nose leather and pads pink. The fur is fine and silky and may be slightly wavy on the stomach. Deafness has been known both in the blue-eyed and odd-eyed varieties since the first Angoras were seen. There is a legend in Turkey that Attaturk will return some day as an odd-eyed deaf Turkish Angora, so the cats there are treated with great respect.

Coloured Angoras have appeared in breeding from some lines and are now being registered by all associations.

These graceful, agile cats with winning ways are playful, affectionate and very communicative with their owners, and seem to retain kittenish behaviour all their lives. They keep themselves very clean, and as the fur is so silky, it mats very little, and grooming is not the problem it can be with some other Longhairs.

Facing page: a Turkish cat. This breed was first brought to Britain in 1955, but as yet is not commonly known in the USA. However, the Turkish Angora (right) has been bred in the USA since 1954, but it is not at the moment commonly known in Britain

Chapter III
The Shorthairs:
Foreign

The Abyssinian

THE Abyssinian is probably the oldest of our foreign Shorthair cat breeds. Interesting and attractive, it is generally assumed that it is the original Egyptian cat; certainly mummified remains have been seen of cats with the colouring peculiar to the Abyssinian. It is known, however, that there were also Blue and Black cats in Ancient Egypt. In Ethiopia the Abyssinian was at one time a prized possession, and was known as the Desert cat because of the 'sand' colour of its coat.

The origin of the Aby (as it is affectionately known in the cat world) is still the subject of great controversy. Many conflicting theories have been put forward by eminent people. Some consider the Aby to be a man-made breed. Others incline to the view expressed by the late Professor HC Brooke (a noted naturalist and an acknowledged authority on cats) that the Abyssinian is descended from the African Caracal lynx which, like the yellow African Kaffir cat, has been known to mate with tame cats and can be domesticated if tamed when young. The Caracal lynx has the reddish coat colour, tufted ears and general expression of the Abyssinian cat.

Other authorities consider Abyssinians are the result of tabby matings and that all stories of their Egyptian and Abyssinian ancestry are purely legend. The factor that gives the greatest weight to this view is that from time to time, kittens of very passable Abyssinian type are born to ordinary tabby parents. Even in the pedigree Abys seen today, tabby markings can occur and are heavily penalized in the show ring. These experts believe that the present-day Abyssinian breed was established by mating carefully selected ticked tabbies of unknown parentage and that the Abyssinian is purely a product of British foundation stock.

Undoubtedly many foreign breeds, especially Siamese, have been bred into the Aby; the original cats of the breed were heavy in build and the Siamese influence has caused the present-day cats to have a lithe and graceful carriage. An 80-year-old painting of an Abyssinian cat with an Indian cat, shows the Aby very much as we know it today with brown ticked coat and green eyes, although the ears are smaller. The Indian cat is larger, with orange eyes and red coat, and white on the mouth, neck and chest.

Called the 'Little Lion' because of its resemblance to the lioness in expression and colour, the early cats were sometimes grey or silver. Harrison Weir, the nineteenth-century authority on cats, writes that he knew of several of these cats imported from Ethiopia before the days of quarantine, when it was quite easy for travellers to bring cats and kittens home by ship. A female named Gondar is recorded in the first Cat Register published in 1898. Very few grey Abys have been seen since the early 1950s, and the browns or normals are now predominant.

It is interesting to quote from Professor Brooke's remarks made in the early 1930s about Abyssinians: 'It is usually assumed that the Egyptian or Caffre cat is the progenitor of the majority of the domestic cats. This is the variety which was domesticated and revered by the Ancient Egyptians. It is easy to understand how, with its eminently tameable disposition, it gradually spread over Europe. Our so-called Abyssinian cats bear a striking resemblance to this handsome type of cat.

A good specimen should very strongly resemble what one might expect the Egyptian cat to become after generations of domestication. The colour of an Aby should be a sort of reddish fawn, each individual hair being ticked like that of a wild rabbit, hence the popular name of bunny cat, and should be a small cat of delicate proportions'.

There is a small stuffed cat, said to be an Aby, in the Leiden Museum, Holland, and thought to have been brought from England before 1882. In the 1950s several kittens of a light red colour appeared in various litters; they were thought to be 'sports' (an animal that differs markedly from the normal) and at first they did not attract much notice. However, some breeders decided to develop the colour; they were gradually improved and in 1963 the Abyssinian Club applied to the Governing Council of the Cat Fancy for the Reds to be recognized as a subsidiary breed. The black ticking on the coat is absent and the colour a solid copper red. The pads and nose are pink.

Today we see many lovely specimens of both colours. A few are shy in the Show pen but most handle well and frequently take Best in Show honours. They make very handsome neuters. Neck rings and leg markings are seldom seen now but the white fur underneath the chin and on the neck – a fault – still persists. A white patch on the chest or stomach, a very definite fault, should debar a cat from winning a championship certificate. The ticked appearance of the Abyssinian's coat is caused by two or three bands of brown or black pigment on every hair. A dark line down the spine is common, and permitted by show judges. Any tabby markings are a serious fault. The inside of the forelegs and belly should be of a tint to harmonize well with the main colour, the preference being given to orange-brown.

The type is foreign but the outline is not so long and svelte as that of the Siamese. The head is not so long and pointed. The body should be long and slender, about 18 inches long, and the tail longish, tapering and whiplike. Eye colour may be green, yellow or hazel. The ears should be sharp, comparatively large and broad at the base. The coat texture should be short, fine and close. The feet are small with black pads. This black colouring extends beyond the paws up the back of the hind legs.

Abyssinians should be owned by people who can give them plenty of space, as they love to climb trees and go hunting.

The normal Abyssinian (right) is darker than the red (left). Originally this breed was heavy in build, but the Siamese influence has made it lithe and graceful

They face hazards when living in the country as they may be mistaken for rabbits and shot or trapped. If kept in towns and allowed to roam they run the risk of being killed on the roads as, once out, they will sometimes stay away for hours.

They are not prolific breeders and usually have small litters of three or four. For some reason more males than females are born, which creates a shortage as females are in great demand. When in season and ready for mating they are quiet 'callers'. The kittens are very attractive and look like little hamsters when very young.

Abys are very independent, very affectionate and intelligent, but not demonstrative unless it suits them. They love their kittens and take excellent care of them. They have the endearing habit of opening and shutting their paws when held up and they have a loud purr. They are now popular in America and several British cats have been exported to the USA. Several very good cats have gone to Australia, where they are in great demand, having their own club and special show in Sydney.

For the last three or four years, efforts have been made to breed Blue and Cream Abyssinians. The Abyssinian Cat Club is not in full agreement about this development, feeling that since so much has been done towards perfecting the Red and Normal breeds, other colours might cause problems. The Club has decided, however, to support the breeding of the new colours, provided they are developed along the lines laid down by the governing bodies, which require three generations of Blue to Blue, and Cream to Cream to be produced before Blue and Cream Abys can be recognized as subsidiary breeds. Several cats of both colours are being produced in America.

Still comparatively rare, Abyssinians are demanding pets, and become restless if kept in close confinement. They make very affectionate companions, and love attention from their owners.

The Burmese

BURMESE cats are in great demand, seriously challenging the Siamese in popularity. They are Shorthairs with a sweet disposition – very active, intelligent, affectionate and loyal. They are capable of performing endearing tricks and get on well both with other cats and with dogs.

Of all breeds of cats the Burmese is probably the only one that does not mind being laughed at. In this respect it differs strikingly from the Siamese. The latter certainly has a sense of humour (not quite the same thing as a sense of fun) but cannot tolerate being teased. Laugh at a Siamese and you are likely to incur its

severe displeasure, and only an apology will restore peace. But a Burmese will laugh with you.

Modern breeds of pedigree cats, generally speaking, have originated in Britain, but the Brown Burmese is an exception to the rule. This breed was established in 1930 in the United States, having been introduced there from India by a Dr J. Thompson of San Francisco. As with the Siamese, however, nobody knows the true origin of the Burmese, despite a variety of ingenious and often fanciful theories. It was recognized in the USA in 1936. In France, the breed is known as Zibelines. There are a number of Brown Burmese on

the Continent, but their rise in popularity has not been so swift as in Britain.

The Brown Burmese Standard requires body colour of even sable-brown, shading to a rather lighter tone on chest and abdomen; the mask, ears, legs and tail must be clearly defined and of a darker brown than the body. The ideal specimen is of medium size, with small oval feet.

Eyes are round, ranging from golden yellow to Chartreuse yellow, with no tendency to squint; ears should be large and wide at the base; the tail should be straight or may slightly kinked at the tip.

When the Burmese was first introduced to Britain from the west coast of the

United States after World War Two, the American Breed Standard was adopted for it and very little alteration has been made to it. For some time, during the 1950s and 1960s, British breeders attempted to introduce a Siamese strain into the Burmese and this resulted in changes to the traditional type, the cats developing longer heads and noses, thinner tails and green or blue-green eyes. These modifications were eventually considered to be undesirable, however, and the Standard of the breed was amended. Green eyes were judged to be faulty and the distinctive 'profile' of the breed had to be emphasized.

Although the breed is foreign in type, the wedge-shaped head is not quite so long as that of the Siamese. In North America, the Standard requires the head of the Burmese to be more rounded and the body shorter, so that the cat is generally more compact and sturdy-looking.

Brown Burmese females should be rather small and dainty, with an average weight of about 8 lb. Occasionally one comes across very much smaller females, but it is not advisable to breed from such cats. Males tend to be larger and elegant.

In the show ring Challenge Certificates are not awarded to Burmese cats with blue or green eyes or with visible kinks in the tail, except at the extreme tip. If an otherwise excellent specimen (particularly an older cat) has a few white hairs, a Challenge Certificate should not necessarily be withheld; but it should never be awarded to a cat with a solid white patch of fur.

Judging the eye colour can present problems, for the apparent shade of Burmese eyes is greatly affected by the colour and intensity of the light in which they are viewed. Ideally they should be judged in moderately strong, diffused daylight. The standard Chartreuse yellow silk ribbon (often supplied by Burmese cat clubs for the assistance of judges) gives a good indication of average Burmese eye colour under such conditions. Comparison with the ribbon is less reliable under artificial light which, to a certain extent, alters the apparent colour of both ribbon and eyes.

In 1955 two Blue kittens appeared in Britain in a litter of Brown Burmese bred by a Mrs Watson. They were registered and the female, Sealcote Blue Surprise, became the progenitor of the Blue variety of the breed. Gradually the Blues were established and in 1960, after three generations of Blue to Blue had been produced, the British Governing Council gave official recognition to the Blue.

For some reason the Blues never gained popularity in the United States and none were imported. So the Burmese Cat Club drew up a Standard of Points which was accepted by the Governing Council of the Cat Fancy. The Blues have rather thicker coats than the Browns and tend to be somewhat longer in the head. Both sexes are, on average, rather heavier than the Browns. The eyes should be lime yellow but may sometimes have dark flecks in them which modify the colour to what can be described as agate. In the early days the eye colour was often a mixture of yellow and blue, referred to as golden turquoise. Although regarded officially as incorrect, the effect was very beautiful. As was the case with the Browns, certain breeders introduced a Siamese strain which also did much to alter the eye colour. The amendment to the Standard of Points referring to the Browns was extended to the Blues, making green eyes a fault in both varieties. The coat of the Blue Burmese is not such a definite blue as that of the Russian and British Blues. It can best be described as resembling the colour of old polished pewter.

In 1970, six Burmese were imported from the west coast of America; four were Chocolate and two were brown, and all carried genes for Chocolate and Lilac colours. As a result these new colours are now being bred in Britain. The Lilacs (known in the USA as platinum), which are pure-bred, have pinkish dove-grey coats with a frosted sheen appearance, and the Chocolates (known in the USA as Champagne) have fur that is pale milk chocolate in colour. Other new colours have appeared during recent years. Through careful planned breeding, a number of pure-bred varieties of Burmese has been produced. These include Cream, with fur of a rich cream colour, which is darker on the face and back and paler on the chest and belly, and Blue-Cream (a female-only variety), whose fur is the same cream, but is mixed with blue. These two have been given subsidiary breed numbers by the Governing Council of the Cat Fancy. (The subsidiary breeds have a Standard of Points, but have not yet been granted championship status.) The colour and markings of Blue-Creams are not as important as their type, which should be excellent, as Blue-Creams are the intermediate step between Browns and Blues on the one hand, and Reds and Creams on the other. Two other new colours are Red, which has rich, golden-red fur shading to a lighter colour on the chest and belly, and Tortie (another female-only variety), with the fur a mixture of red, brown and cream. Standards and breed numbers have not yet been granted. Type is good for all these varieties, and it is to be hoped that they become as popular as the Brown and Blue Burmese.

The Brown Burmese (centre) is a recent addition to the Cat Fancy. Even newer colours include Cream (top left), Blue (right) and Blue Cream (below)

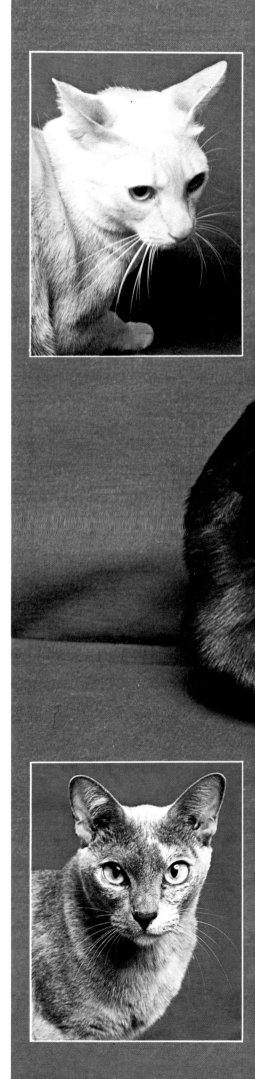

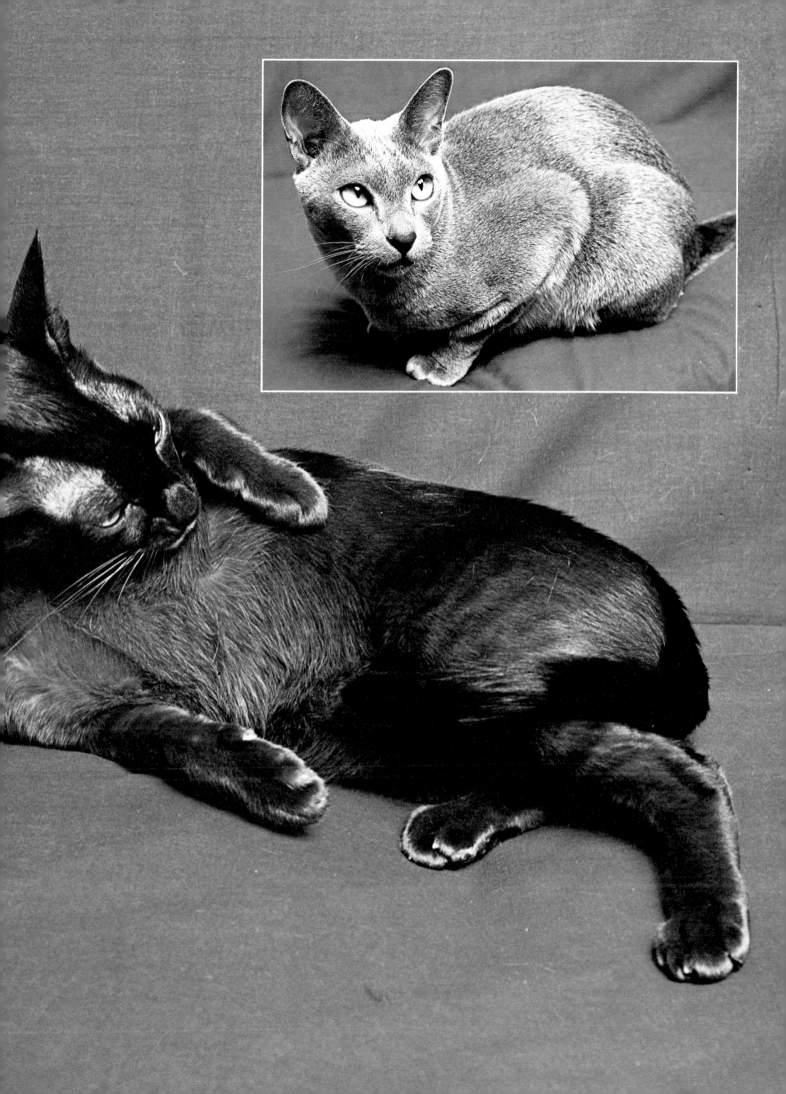

The Devon and Cornish Rex

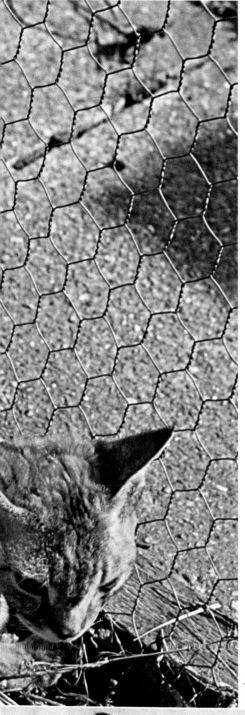

THE Rex coat was first noticed in a cat by a woman called Mrs Ennismore, in Cornwall in 1956. The matter was brought to the attention of Dr A G Searle, who wrote a paper on the subject for the *Journal of Genetics*. The cats concerned had wavy fur and curved whiskers and eyebrows. They were taken up by the late Brian Stirling-Webb, our foremost experimental cat breeder, and a group of his friends. The original Cornish Rex stud cat was given the delightful name of Kallibunker. Its coat was cream-and-white, and it had long legs and a head that was a little longer than those of domestic shorthairs.

Not long after the discovery of the Cornish Rex, a cat with wavy fur was brought to Mr Stirling-Webb from Devon. This was a male cat named Kirlee, and who was duly welcomed by the group of early Rex breeders and mated to their queens. Unfortunately, they soon had a shock, as Cornish Rex mated to Devon Rex produced only normal short-haired kittens. It was soon found, however, that these Shorthairs, mated between themselves, gave a percentage of Rex-coated kittens. Owners proceeded with breeding the cats, even though they realized that Cornish Rex and Devon Rex were not compatible, as the two genes which caused wavy fur were not the same. They soon discovered that in the second generation after a Devon-Cornish cross, Devon genes

The coat of the Devon Rex (left) is short, fine, wavy and soft; that of the Cornish Rex (below) is short and plushy

might pair with Devon genes, or Cornish with Cornish, and whenever this happened, a wavy-coated kitten would be born.

Later it was decided to breed the two varieties of Rex cats separately, and two Standards of Points were drawn up. These were altered once or twice, and the British Governing Council of the Cat Fancy in due course approved them as provisional standards and later granted the Rex cats recognition and championship status.

Unfortunately, the Devons were found to have a destructive factor in their genetic make-up which produced hairlessness; they had bare patches on their chests, necks, legs and underparts, and one kitten was born completely furless. Although this was plainly undesirable, those who were taken with the variety would not give up. Devon Rex cats have peculiarly attractive heads, with big, low-set ears, plump cheeks and short faces, so that they have a 'pixie' look. Their owners breed them with very great care, and some beautiful cats, with thick, lovely coats, have appeared at shows. This has been achieved by the time-honoured method of selection, in this case by mating together the individuals with the best coats. There has also been an introduction of Longhair blood, resulting in a lovely cat called Briarry Waitrose, whose descendants have done much to eliminate the undesired hairlessness.

Besides these two varieties, there were Rex cats in the United States, where wavy-coated cats were first seen many years ago and were named Karakul. Both Cornish and Devon Rex cats were exported to America. A Rex queen was also found in Germany at approximately the same time as the appearance of the Cornish Rex. The work of Charlie and Mable Tracy of the USA and some of their friends has proved that Cornish Rex and German Rex are compatible: that is to say that mated together they will have only Rex kittens. This is a very good thing, for the German Rex constitutes a splendid outcross as it has only recently come from free cat populations living on farmland, and all specimens are healthy. To inbreed the Rex in order to preserve its appearance would eventually ruin its health and fail in its purpose, so that the fact that they exist in various parts of the world, and that some of the strains are compatible, is extremely important.

The wavy coats are so unusual that it is sometimes thought that they are different from other cats, but this is not so. For instance, the idea has been put forward that these cats require extra fat, and must be given a small amount of suet to eat each day. The reason for this idea is that Rex cats have no guard hairs and, in the case of Cornish and German, no awn hairs either. Their pelage (coat) is made up entirely of down hairs – the underfur which, in an ordinary shorthair, is covered by overfur consisting of awn hairs and guard hairs – and people have thought that without guard hairs the cats would feel cold and need extra fat in their diet. However, there are Cornish Rex whose coats are so thick that it is impossible to find the skin, and it must be remembered that these cats – even Devons with a measure of hairlessness – have maintained themselves in the wild. This they could not have done if they were insufficiently protected from the cold. Their meals should not be different from those of other cats. They should be given fresh raw heart, plain boiled white fish, and all the kinds of food that are good for a domestic cat.

Rex cats, because they have such large ears, are perhaps more likely to have them torn should any fighting take place between the males during the mating season. Every wound needs to be bathed in warm water to which a mild disinfectant has been added. If the wound is serious, it may need to be stitched. This, of course, is a matter for your veterinary surgeon.

Cat's ears usually stay remarkably clean and may need no attention whatsoever

These Devon Rex kittens display pixie look of the breed, with big low-set ears, plump cheeks and short faces

from their owner. But cleaning becomes necessary when ear disease develops. The ear, being such a delicate organ, is liable to be damaged if the person cleaning the ear is not an expert. It is best to leave it to the skill of the vet, unless he has shown you how to go about the task. Often the indication that a cat has severe ear trouble is in its walk. It may walk as if drunk, or in circles, or may even have a fit. Professional advice should be sought immediately if this occurs.

A good Rex coat, rippling in firm waves from neck to tail-tip, is so unusual and beautiful that the cats have travelled all over the world, and there are classes for them at shows not only in Europe and the USA but in New Zealand, Australia, South Africa and many other countries. In Britain, Rex cats are catered for by the Colourpoint, Rex and the Any Other Variety Club and by the Rex Cat Club.

Grooming them is not difficult. It is a simple matter to prepare a Rex cat for a show, and it can best be done if daily attention has been paid to the coat as a matter of routine. Every cat needs to have its eyes and ears regularly inspected; in the case of Rex a very little flea powder of a reputable make rubbed daily with the fingertips into the fur, especially where tail and back meet, will keep the cat free from these parasites. This powder can be used every day from birth, but only a very little is needed at a time. With a show in prospect, it should not be used for a couple of days and never on the day of the show, for powder found in an exhibit's coat leads to disqualification.

An excellent lotion is sold at good chemists for application to feline fur, and this, put on with the hands, will make the waves of fur shine. One breeder puts almond oil on her champion's crinkly

whiskers before a show; gentle strokes with a chamois leather, following the lines of the waves, gives finish to the appearance of the coat. It is, really, the coat which is, as one of the American Standards states, 'The singular and most important feature' of a Rex cat. It is fascinating to see new-born Rex kittens, with their ridged fur, as if they were wearing little purl-plain suits. Their coats apart, however, these cats do not differ greatly from felines of other breeds. In character, there are no two exactly alike, but all have a measure of intelligence. There is one Rex which will fetch – always from the same place – toys for her kittens to play with; some will hide favoured playthings in a 'hidey-hole', for future use.

These cats make charming pets; as a rule, they have equable temperaments. In judging, it is possible to encounter, probably latish in the day, an exhibit which is scared by its strange surroundings and which has 'had enough' and will not be handled; it would be very unusual to find a Rex cat, however, which could not be judged at a show. There are some – and it is fair to say that this applies to other breeds too – which seem to positively rejoice in the admiration which they get at shows. Two Rex cats were shown once which, presumably because they were bored, slept comfortably throughout the day, and thus were not of great interest to spectators! This evenness of temper makes the little Rex cats ideal pets; they like their homes, their owners, the pleasant routine that is theirs when they have the 'right' humans to look after them. These cats with their striking, multi-coloured fur, can win at shows for their owners and – better still – can be delightful friends and companions to the people who love them.

The Havana

THE Havana Cat, known in the USA as the Havana Brown, is the self-coloured equivalent of the Chocolate Point Siamese. (By 'self' is meant the same colour all over with no pattern.) In Britain the main points of the Standard are as follows: it must be identical in type and conformation to the Siamese, with long svelte body lines, medium in size, lithe and well muscled. The tail is long and whip-like, and the legs long and slender, with the hind legs being slightly longer than the forelegs. The long and well-proportioned head narrows to a fine muzzle and is topped by large pointed ears, wide at the base and with little hair.

The paws are small and oval and the pads of the feet and the nose leather are a distinctive pinkish colour. The coat may be any shade of rich, chestnut brown, somewhat darker than the Burmese. It must be short and glossy, even and sound throughout, and the well-set eyes must be slanting and distinctly oriental in type, and a definite green. Faults are considered to be tabby and other markings, dark or shadow points (as are sometimes seen in the young Burmese), white spots or hairs, a cobby shape, round head, a short, thick or kinked tail, and crossed eyes. Its full title is the Havana Foreign.

In the American Standard for the breed there are several differences, calling for a cat of unique type, quite distinguishable from the Siamese, and with all features only moderately accentuated. The main difference between the American Havana Brown and the Havana of Britain is in the head, as the American Standard calls for a rounded muzzle with an indentation on either side of the face behind the whisker pads. In profile there must be a distinct 'stop' at the eyes, and the end of the muzzle should be almost square. American show rules penalize their Havana Brown cats for lack of stop, weak chin, pointed ears, eyes either too oriental or too round, body either too cobby or too rangy, and a melanistic or coarse-textured coat. In Britain, however, under the rules of the Governing Council of the Cat Fancy, an Havana would be penalized for showing white hairs, having any yellow or blue tinge in the eye-colour or deviating from the Siamese type.

The earliest record of a self brown cat is dated 1894, when an Englishwoman, Mrs French, imported a queen called Granny Grumps and her son Master Timkey Brown, described by a contemporary writer as Siamese cats with coats of burnished Chestnut and green-blue eyes. Three Swiss Mountain Cats, also purported to be chocolate 'selfs' were im-

The Havana cat is very similar to the Siamese. Both breeds have long, svelte body lines and a long, whip-like tail

This and facing page: Havana kittens are perhaps the most forward of all breeds. They open their eyes on the third or fourth day, and purr, crawl and eat well in advance of other breeds. Facing page, below: a Havana queen displaying the typical alertness and feline grace of the breed

ported at the turn of the century, and one called Sin Li was to have founded a strain but unfortunately died before siring any kittens. Other imports were made, but it is not clear whether these were Chocolate Selfs or Brown Burmese, and at that time little was understood about the differences in their genetic make-up.

Very little was done to develop self brown cats, possibly because of the lack of knowledge of the laws of genetics appertaining to the Siamese and Burmese breeds. If a Burmese Brown were mated to a Chocolate-Self Siamese, only black kittens would have resulted, and this was a most disappointing conclusion for the breeder of the early part of the century.

In 1951, however, the Baroness von Ull-man, having studied basic colour inheritance in the cat, decided to try to produce Chocolate Selfs. She carried out preliminary matings between her Chocolate Point Siamese stud male and a black cat of foreign type. She also contacted a Mrs Armitage Hargreaves of Devon, who set up her own breeding programme using Siamese and Russian Blue cats. Meanwhile, another breeder, Mrs Munro-Smith of Reading, was trying to produce Colourpoint Persians, and from a mismating between her Black Longhair female and a Seal Point Siamese, resulted some black

female kittens. One of these was mated back to her Siamese grandfather as an experiment, and in her litter was one self-brown male. This first chocolate brown male kitten was born in late 1952. This was Elmtower Bronze Idol, the famous progenitor of the breed. Other fanciers became enamoured of these cats with their burnished mahogany coats and emerald eyes, and before long several distinct breeding lines were established. In 1956 the first breeding pair crossed the Atlantic to California and established the Havana in the USA. By 1958, with three clear generations of like-to-like matings behind them, the Havana was officially recognized in Britain and given full championship status.

A great controversy arose because it was felt that the name 'Havana' would cause confusion in the minds of the public at large with the Havana rabbit, bred mainly for its fur. So the Governing Council of the Cat Fancy decided to give the breed the name of the Chestnut Brown Foreign Shorthair, and so it was known until 1970. Then this unwieldy title was revoked and the breed once again became known as the Havana.

The first Havana to be made a champion was in the early 1960s. Then numbers dwindled alarmingly until it was rare to find a self Chocolate on the show bench. However, in 1965, a new wave of enthusiasts took up this attractive variety and since then it has become increasingly popular. The new lines are of extremely good type and stamina, not only winning in breed classes but the top show awards also, including Best in Show and Grand Challenge certificates.

Calm and even in temperament, the Havana makes the ideal show cat. There are no prima donna tendencies in this breed, although some, especially stud males, like to act clownishly from time to time. Extremely affectionate and often bursting with vitality, the Havana is a joy to live with, not least because it is always aesthetically pleasing.

Havana cats will always reward their owners if they are given a little extra care and attention. A good, well-balanced diet, high in protein and fats, gives a bloom to the coat that can never be equalled by grooming, and plenty of exercise ensures that the muscles are kept in hard condition at all times. The careful selection of breeding stock in the modern Havana has ensured that congenital defects are practically non-existent. This breed seems particularly immune to upper respiratory infections and show fever.

Structural defects, such as kinked tails, projecting sternum and poor dentition, so prevalent in the Siamese, are rarely seen in the Havana. These cats make excellent breeding stock, maturing early, having easy parturition and making excellent mothers. The kittens are always very forward, opening their eyes on the third or fourth day, crawling, purring and eating well ahead of the average time. Being highly intelligent and quick to take advantage of any situation, careful training from an early age is necessary to prevent the Havana from dominating the household. Most Havanas adapt well to entirely indoor living, making them ideal pets for flat-dwellers. Grooming the Havana presents no problems, for the best way to keep its coat immaculate is by hand-stroking every day. This tones up the muscles and gives a wonderful shine to the fur. Each week its claws should be inspected and if necessary shortened with nail clippers, and the inside of the ear flaps should be wiped clean of grease. For show purposes, a soft dry chamois leather or silk scarf is employed to buff the coat still further. Male cats may need an occasional bath to remove grease from the sebaceous glands at the base of the tail. Damp fingers massaged into the coat remove dead hair during the spring and autumn moult. The dead hair can then be groomed out with a fine-toothed comb.

The interests of the Havana owner are now being promoted by the Havana Club. In the comparatively short time this club has been in existence its membership—drawn from all over the United Kingdom—has risen to above 100, and soon it is hoped that affiliation will be granted by the Governing Council of the Cat Fancy. Through the efforts of the club officials and members, what was a 'dead' breed in the Cat Fancy from about 1950 to 1965 has taken on a new lease of life. From 1965

onwards, interest has grown continuously, and now the Havana Club is able to offer to its members – and to newcomers who wish to own a Havana specimen – breeding advice, a stud and kitten list, and the opportunity to win club rosettes, club 'specials' and points that go towards club trophies at cat shows.

The Havana is a remarkably hardy breed, and breeders who keep a careful watch on their veterinary bills say that those for the Havana are extremely low. In fact they are generally regarded as slightly more hardy than the Siamese. The queens give birth easily, 'getting on with the job', and demand the minimum of attention from owners. The kittens are easy to wean, and quickly show a preference for solids.

A favourable trait of the Havana springs from its relationship with its owner. This has been described by enthusiastic Havana owners as 'dog-like', the phrase being intended as a compliment. The Havana is fanatically devoted to its owner. It likes going for walks with him or her, just as a pet dog does, and will either follow behind or will accept being led on a lead.

It is not surprising, with these virtues of the breed becoming more widely known as a result of the activities of the Havana Club, that this relative newcomer to the British Cat Fancy is rapidly increasing in popularity. As more and more people succumb to the charms of the Havana, it is becoming more difficult to find kittens exactly when they are wanted. But it is well worth joining the waiting list of a reputable breeder in order to get a well-reared, well-bred specimen.

The Russian Blue

THIS is a cat for the connoisseur. It belongs to an old, beautiful and comparatively rare breed that has enjoyed limited popularity during the last 80 years. Russian Blues probably originated in Russia and were at first called 'Archangel' cats. From 1880 onwards, until quarantine laws were introduced in Britain, several were imported to this country, and early records describe their thick, seal-like coats which were their natural protection against the very cold Russian climate. These cats were also found in the Scandinavian countries, where a few still flourish. They were imported from Archangel in Russia by sailors and travellers. However, cats with blue fur have also been called Spanish, Maltese, or American cats.

Very few Russian Blues have been imported into Britain during the last 30 years and numbers have gradually declined. They are not prolific breeders and therefore not a good proposition for anyone with keen business instincts. So many breeds of pedigree cat are now recognized in Britain and in North America that the Russian Blue has many rivals, although fortunately there are still enough people interested in them to prevent them from vanishing entirely.

From notes made in 1889 by Harrison Weir, an acknowledged expert, it would appear that many were imported into Britain in the late nineteenth century, when it was quite easy to bring them by ship from the Scandinavian countries. They were also called Spanish Blue, and Chartreuse Blue. Harrison Weir did not believe they were a distinct breed, but were a light-coloured form of the black cat. He knew of one in particular which was a beautiful blue colour slightly tinged with purple. It was exhibited at one of the early Crystal Palace shows in London, and was the offspring of a Tabby and White female and a Black and White male. He presumed that this was a British hybrid.

He drew up the first Standard for the breed in 1889, for his own guidance. It suggested that the coat should be even in colour, of a bluish-lilac tint, with no sootiness or black; green eyes were specified, with black pads and a black nose. He remarked that if Russians were crossed with British Blue cats (which were usually found on farms) the coat might be a light blue-grey; the nose and pads would often be of a deep chocolate colour, and the eyes yellow. He added, however, that the cats that came direct from Archangel were a deeper, purer colour than the cross-breeds; they also had larger ears (which were more transparent than those of the British-bred cat) and were longer in the head and legs. The coat tended to be very short and thick but also extremely bright and glossy. Today's Standards are still based on Harrison Weir's description. It is interesting to note that some of the first important 'Archangel' cats were blue and white, or white.

The earliest registrations in the years 1898 to 1899 show that a Mr. Brooks imported a white Russian female, no name given; another white Russian was registered as 'Granny'. There was also 'Olga', a Russian Blue with a white spot. Undoubtedly other cats were brought in which were not registered, and some were interbred with the British Blue. They were shown together in classes for 'Blues', but the type was not stated. It is probably safe to assume that 'Prince Romanoff', 'Meehka', 'Songa' and 'Nicolaivitch' were of foreign type, and 'Blue Thomas' and 'Cathcart Blue Lad' were of British type, but all were in one class.

In 1912 Mr C. A. House, one of the first officially appointed cat judges in Britain, wrote of the breed: 'Years ago, cats of distinctive character came to this country from Russia, being usually brought over by the crews of vessels trading between Archangel and our north-eastern ports. Eventually they were recognized by the Council as Russian Blues. These cats had the Eastern type of face and were lithe and slim in body. They all had green eyes and the texture of their coat was like unto plush. In every detail they were unlike our British cats.'

By the time the third British Stud Book was published in 1927, the British and Foreign Blues were separated, and this register records seven males and twenty-one females of foreign type, far outnumbering the British Blue.

In type, Russian Blue cats are quite different from the British Blue, having longer, thinner bodies, long and narrow tails, green eyes, slender legs, small oval feet and prominent whisker pads. The coat should ideally be very short, silky and of a medium-blue shade. Unfortunately, this type of coat is nowadays very rare; colour is usually good but the characteristic seal-like texture is rarely seen. Recently, a young male Russian Blue was found wandering in Aberdeen, having apparently strayed off a boat. It was evidently a pet, as it was well grown

The beautiful Russian Blue is a graceful animal with a unique double coat which is blue with a silvery sheen

and very friendly. It conformed to the description of the original Russian Blue and was a lovely cat, with beautiful green eyes and a dark blue coat of the texture of a baby seal. This coat would be necessary in very cold climates but, as we know, the density and shiny seal-like appearance is gradually lost if the animal lives permanently in a warmer climate. This is, in fact, what has happened to the Aberdeen cat. Now a lovely neuter, it has developed a coat of much softer texture.

It is most important, when breeding, not to mate Russian Blues with British Blues, Blue Burmese or Blue-Pointed Siamese, unless the breeding is very strictly controlled, as all these cats have their own personality and type. This is known as 'outcrossing'. Some years ago Blue-Pointed Siamese were outcrossed with Russian Blues and although type in both breeds benefited, difficulties were experienced with eye colour and, perhaps most important of all, the voice. The Siamese voice is notoriously penetrating and demanding but the Russian Blue voice is almost non-existent. Whereas it was rather disconcerting to hear a Russian cat calling loudly, it was a novelty to find a Blue-Pointed Siamese with no voice!

Special distinguishing features of the Russian Blue are their prominent whisker pads; they stand out like pincushions and are very distinctive. The true Russian Blue cat should have large, thinly-furred ears; unfortunately many cats today have ears that are too small. Another feature all have in common is their small, silvery feet, which are shown to perfection in the small dainty females.

The Russian Blue has much to recommend it. It is an easy cat to manage, it has a 'small' voice and it is not unusually demanding. When the coat is of a good colour and the eyes a definite bright green, it is a lovely animal. The breed is quiet and clean and has a good constitution. It is rather shy, home-loving and affectionate, and will walk on a lead. Despite a superficial resemblance, there is no cause to confuse it with the Blue Burmese, as the type, colour of eyes and texture of the coat are quite different.

Russian Blues are not prolific breeders, the average number of kittens in a litter being three or four. Queens usually have their kittens without trouble (perhaps their placid nature helps), and they are good mothers. The kittens are very sweet, but these cats should live in quiet homes as they respond most readily to gentle and soft-voiced people, and are seen at their best in such surroundings. The males are bigger than the females; when type is good they are handsome and elegant cats and can be extremely companionable pets when neutered.

Russian Blue cats are a challenge to breeders for it is very difficult to breed to the Standard. The basic problems are to produce the snake-like head and large, rather transparent ears. Apart from over-small ears, most Russian Blues tend to be too heavy. Coat colour and texture, however, are often very good, and the eyes continue to be a good green.

The interests of the Russian Blues in Britain are guarded by a specialist club, the Short-haired Cat Society of Great Britain, formed in 1901. It elects judges for the various short-haired breeds and is responsible for any alterations to the Standard. The first Standard was approved by the Society in 1902 and it stated that coat colour should be a bright blue, pale or medium shades being preferred to dark blue. Eye colour was required to be orange or amber. These points were modified in a new Standard drawn up in 1910. In July 1966, another Standard was drawn up by the Short-haired Cat Society, in agreement with certain continental clubs, and approved by the Governing Council of the Cat Fancy. This states that the Russian Blue should be a clear blue colour, even throughout, and, in maturity, free from tabby markings or shadings. A medium blue colour is preferred. The coat

The Russian Blue of today has been produced by carefully planned breeding

should be short, thick and very fine, standing up soft and silky like seal skin. The coat is double which gives it a distinct silvery sheen. The tail should be fairly long and tapering. The Russian Blue should have long legs and small oval feet. The head should be a short wedge shape, with a flat skull and a straight forehead and nose. Whisker pads should be prominent. Eyes should be a vivid green, set rather wide apart and almond-shaped. The ears should be large and pointed, wide at the base and set vertically to the head. The skin of the ears should be thin and transparent, with very little hair inside the ears. Major faults are white or tabby markings; cobby or heavy build; square head; yellow in eyes.

Russian Blues are popular in Australia, and a very good strain has been bred there from exported English stock. The breed has a limited appeal in America, where it is often known as the Maltese or American Blue, and type resembles the Siamese. They also have a Blue rival in the Korat cat; again type is different. Although the coat colour may be similar, both texture and eye colour are quite different.

The Siamese

THE phenomenal success of the Siamese cat is due largely to its unusual nature. It is exceptionally affectionate; as a kitten it plays more vigorously than most other breeds; as an adult it displays great intelligence; and as a neutered pet it is a delightful companion. Nevertheless, it made its initial impact on the western world because of its spectacular appearance. Brought to Britain towards the end of the nineteenth century, the cats immediately became extremely popular. It was not until the early 1900s that they were seen in America. The combination of a creamy coat as smooth as ermine, dense seal points and vivid blue eyes was unusual and striking, and the discovery that the cats had unusually forthcoming temperaments added to their great charm. In view of this it was not at all surprising that they should rapidly become the most popular of all cat breeds.

A considerable amount of research has been carried out into the origin of the Siamese cat. Several theories have been advanced, but no definite conclusions reached. What we do know however, is that the breed came to Europe from Siam. There, for generations, members of the breed were royal cats living at the palace of the King of Siam in Bangkok. They were not allowed to live anywhere else and were very closely guarded.

This stringent rule was waived in 1884 when the British Consul-General at Bangkok was permitted to bring a pair of Siamese cats to Britain. This was their first appearance in Europe and the beautiful creatures created quite a stir. The following year saw the importation of a pair into France from Siam. The first pair seen in America was thought to have been a present from the King of Siam to an American friend.

The great admiration which most people have for the Siamese springs from a combination of factors. It is elegantly proportioned, its eyes are of a striking colour and shape, and there is great delicacy in the colours of its coat. But perhaps its most striking and endearing characteristic is the devotion and loyalty it displays towards its owner.

The Siamese is also highly intelligent, apt to be destructive, and extremely vocal. Owners claim to be able to identify a number of different 'miaows', each with a special meaning. At times the voice of the Siamese is shrill and raucous; quite out of keeping with its elegant appearance.

There are seven varieties of Siamese cat recognized by the Governing Council of the Cat Fancy, but whatever the variety, the type is the same. The Siamese is a glossy Shorthair; its fur is fine and lies closely on a medium-sized body that can best be described as svelte. Its feet are small and oval in shape and its legs are slim, the hind legs being a shade higher than those in front, giving the breed a distinctive walk. The long head is wide between the eyes and it narrows in absolutely straight lines to the small muzzle. The ears are pricked and wide at the base. Undoubtedly the brilliant deep blue eyes with an oriental slant are a compelling feature of the breed. They shine red in the dark whereas the eyes of other cats shine green. Another attractive feature is its straight tapering tail (in which a slight kink is permitted in the Breed Standard).

The body colour contrasts with that of the points in all varieties. The Seal Point has a cream body and seal-brown points; The Blue Point is a glacial white with blue shadings on the back, and has blue points; the Chocolate Point has an ivory-coloured coat and milk-chocolate points; the Lilac Point is magnolia in colour with pinkish-grey points; the Red Point is white merging into apricot on the back, with reddish-gold points; the Tortie Point (invariably an all-female variety) can be cream or fawn, the mask marbled with seal, cream and red, and the ears seal colour with red but no cream; the Tabby Point is pale

on the body with no markings, and the ears are a solid colour with no stripes, but the mask has clearly defined stripes with cheek markings. The legs of the Tabby Point should be marked with broken stripes, (with solid markings on the backs of the hind legs and no markings on the feet), and the tail ringed with a solid tip.

Siamese are usually very fond of raw meat, although there are cats which will not eat it unless it is cooked. Grated carrots and cooked chicory can be added if the cat accepts these vegetables. Some Siamese enjoy chicory very much, and this has the added attraction for the owner of being an antidote to constipation and of helping to prevent the formation of hair-balls. A spoonful of olive oil once a week–which the cat will probably enjoy–is a good hair-ball preventive.

Oil is present, of course, in such fish as brisling, pilchards and sardines, which most cats like. However, a diet consisting entirely of fish should be avoided and too much white fish it certainly inadvisable, as such a diet is thought to be a cause of skin complaints. As a general rule the cat's meal, either meat or fish, should be served dry. Experience has shown that the cat's digestion suffers if a milky meal is taken shortly after a meal course. Three or more hours should be allowed to elapse between the two.

The Siamese are extremely clean cats. Owners should therefore pay them the compliment of seeing that they live in the

most hygienic conditions. Although a cat bought from a breeder is almost certain to be house-trained, it is advisable to have a sanitary tray inside the house. This, filled with dry earth or peat-moss litter, should be kept always in the same place so that the cat knows where to go in an emergency.

Because the Siamese cat is a Shorthair it is not as likely to suffer from hair-balls as a long-haired cat. Nevertheless, the fact that the Siamese is so clean and spends

Below and left (bottom): Seal Point are the most popular of all the Siamese varieties. Left (above) a Tabby Point Siamese

so much time on its toilet means that it licks its coat much more than the average Shorthair. There is, therefore, the possibility of it swallowing enough loose hair to form a blockage; this is particularly likely during the spring moulting season.

The owner can help to prevent this by brushing and combing the cat. Most Siamese relish this kind of attention. The loose hairs are removed first by a fine steel comb and then the coat is brushed from head to tail. A few drops of an approved non-poisonous disinfectant in water should be used about once every ten days as a dip for the comb; in hot weather this helps to free the cat from

fleas. The coat of a Siamese in good health should be close-lying and faintly scented, reminiscent of sandalwood.

Over the years, the Siamese has adapted itself to more temperate climates. However, during very cold weather the Siamese owner should provide some extra warmth for his pet.

The owner of a newly acquired Siamese can be certain that he or she has a delightful companion and friend. The kitten will, of course, be a responsibility, for in addition to its basic needs, such as being fed and groomed, it will be demanding of your time and affection. But in return it will give you its lifelong devotion.

Breeding the Siamese

Siamese Seal Point kittens at eight weeks. This breed is the most popular one because of its outstanding appearance and its affectionate nature

ONE worrying factor to the first owners of the Siamese was that the cats seemed to be delicate. At the beginning of this century there was no cure for feline infectious enteritis or for the various forms of cat influenza, so cats of all breeds succumbed to these distress- ing illnesses. Owners of Siamese, suspect- ing that their cats must have picked up scraps of meat impregnated with poison, kept their pets confined to house and garden, carefully supervising everything they ate. Yet this did not prevent the loss of most, if not all, of their cats and kittens. The death rate among cats was reduced dramatically after the discovery of penicil- lin, and subsequent advances in the field of veterinary science during the 1930s and 1940s made it possible for reliable vac- cines to be produced which prevented these diseases altogether. The growing

Siamese Fancy then felt more secure. Large litters were reared, British breeders sent cats to their American counterparts, and then Siamese from both countries were exported to Europe, Australia, New Zealand and South Africa. It was realized that Siamese cats were no more delicate than any others, and the Fancy settled down to develop the breed.

On both sides of the Atlantic, breeders were united in their aims. The early Siamese had heads that were longer than those of domestic Shorthairs, and more slender bodies. They tended, too, to have eyes that were oriental in shape. These were characteristics admired by owners. The kinks to be seen in the tails of certain Siamese were recognized as being defects and were gradually eliminated by selective breeding. By mating together cats with exceptionally long heads, individuals have been born with knife-like faces and receding lower jaws; but this undesirable characteristic can be corrected by careful choice in breeding.

Breeders of Siamese have lately been conspicuously successful in producing new points' colours. Early breeders found that occasionally a kitten would be born with points that were not the traditional seal colour, but either brown or blue. The Chocolate (brown) Points were at first frowned upon, but Blue Points were an immediate success. They were recognized by the governing bodies, and classes were arranged for them at shows. The Chocolate Points took much longer to come into their own, but once they were established, geneticists were quick to realize that crossing a Chocolate Point with a Blue Point would produce, in the second generation, a Lilac Point. All these colours, at their best, are extremely beautiful. The original Seal Points, with the strong contrast between their creamy coat and deep, dense points, are perhaps still the favourites, but the pastel shades are undeniably beautiful and have many devotees. One advantage of the Chocolates and Lilacs is that, because of a special pigmentation factor, their coats remain pale longer than do those of Seals and Blues. Whereas a large Seal Point kitten has a complete mask by the time it is three months old, as well as colour on its paws and tail, a Chocolate Point may not acquire fully coloured points until adulthood. On the other hand, the volatile brown quality will not spread to the coat as the cat grows older, as so often occurs in a Seal or a Blue Point.

When kittens are born they are white or off-white, with no colour appearing in the coat and points (mask, ears, legs, feet and tail) until they are about three weeks old. Some experts believe that the basic colour of the coat can be influenced by diet and the temperature of the environment and that cats fed exclusively on a meat diet and kept in an overheated environment have dark coloured coats and points.

In the 1940s and 1950s Dr Norah Archer in Britain and Mrs da Felippo in the USA bred a number of Red Point kittens, and during the same period Tabby Point Siamese began to appear at shows. They were bred by the introduction of red from a Shorthair Red Self and a Red Tabby respectively. The pale coats are maintained by breeding back, now and then, to a Seal Point, in order to avoid producing Siamese-shaped cats with tabby or marmalade coats.

Because the USA is so vast, there are many governing bodies of the Cat Fancy. Some of these do not accept the Red Points as Siamese (although judging them by the Siamese Standard) but call them

The Tabby Point Siamese, like all varieties of Siamese, is a beautiful animal

Colourpoints. This is confusing for the European cat-lover who has come to recognize the Colourpoint as a separate Longhair breed with Siamese coat pattern, originally bred by the late Brian Stirling-Webb. In the USA the British Colourpoint is known as the Himalayan. Other American governing bodies, such as the Crown Cat Fanciers' Federation, do acknowledge the Red Points as Siamese.

It is arguable that the introduction of red, which brought this variety into being, is no different from the introduction of blue (probably from a self-blue cat akin to the Malay or Korat) which occurred perhaps thousands of years ago and resulted in the Blue Point Siamese. Cats are no respecters of frontiers, and it is fair to assume that there was, in the distant past, a movement of feline populations among the eastern countries, of which Thailand is one. Consequently, the black cat, whose temperature mechanism permitted its colour to show only in its cooler extremities, could mix freely with the blue cat from Korat or with the brown cat from Burma, which is similar to the modern Burmese breed.

Although the Red Points usually possess wonderful type and ermine-like coats, their points are often incomplete. Sometimes the mask and ears will be excellent but the 'gloves' and 'stockings' so pale

as to be almost non-existent. In this respect, Scandinavia and New Zealand have an advantage as in these countries many Red Points have their full complement of golden red markings.

It has been claimed that the Tabby Point Siamese is the most beautiful Siamese breed of all, and undoubtedly it is one of the most unusual and attractive. For this reason it is worth considering in detail the history of its development.

Its mask, stockings and tail are striped and its brilliant blue eyes are outlines with matching colour. As in all Siamese breeds, its general body colour is a creamy beige. It has been developed from crosses between domestic tabbies and Seal Point Siamese, and the majority of the contemporary Tabby Points descend from two famous cats known as Patti and Miss Tee Kat. Both these cats were mated to top quality Seal Point Siamese and from their progeny have evolved many prizewinners.

The history of the Tabby Point is intriguing for, although it was described in the very early days of the Cat Fancy and was scientifically bred during the 1920s, none of the cats bred today descend from these pedigrees. Silver Points were reported in the 1940s but, although there is no doubt that these were tabby, it seems likely that they were Silver Tabby Point rather than the Seal Tabby Point later bred from Patti and Miss Tee Kat.

The breeding scheme followed by the Tabby Point pioneers was to mate the Tabby Points of each successive generation back to top quality Siamese and by this means a proportion of the kittens bred were Tabby Point with each generation better than the last. By 1966 the Tabby Points excelled in all the qualities of the Siamese, and in Britain the Governing Council of the Cat Fancy granted them a special breed number (Breed 32).

During the early years of its development, the Tabby Point Siamese was described variously as Silver Point, Shadow Point, Lynx Point, Attabiy Point and Tabby Point. Finally the British chose the latter name, while in America it was called the Lynx Point.

The name Tabby Point is prefixed by the appropriate colour name–Seal Tabby Point; Blue Tabby Point; Chocolate Tabby Point; Lilac Tabby Point; Red Tabby Point; Cream Tabby Point and Tortie-Tabby Point. The Tortie-Tabby Point varieties are further sub-divided into Seal Tortie-Tabby Point, Blue Tortie-Tabby Point; Chocolate Tortie-Tabby Point and Lilac Tortie-Tabby Point. The Tortie-Tabby Points show mottled tortoiseshell markings as well as tabby stripes. They are valuable for the wide range of colour and pattern varieties they can produce but, probably because of their rather indeterminate appearance they do not

The Seal Point Siamese (above and facing page, top) was the original Siamese from which the other colours have been bred. It is still the most popular variety. The more recent Blue Point (facing page, bottom), is also a beautiful cat

often attain top show honours.

The original Tabby Point colour was Seal–a cat with its mask, stockings and tail striped or ringed with hairs that are banded in sepia-black and buff. Ideally the colour on the trunk should be cream, but it is usual for shading of sepia to appear at maturity or even before. The darkening of its body colour shows traces of banded hairs and tabby pattern. The Blue Tabby Point has hairs banded in slate blue-grey and buff. The general body colour is a slightly greyer shade of cream. The Chocolate Tabby Point has striping made up of hair banded in chocolate brown and a warm, almost orange buff. The effect is more cinnamon than chocolate. The colour striping of the Lilac Tabby Point is made up of hairs banded in a faded lilac and beige so that the final effect is of muted stripes on an almost white body colour. Red and Cream Tabby Points are rarely exhibited.

Recent breeding tests have produced a number of new Siamese varieties and one of these has been identified as the Silver. The colour names are Silver Seal Tabby

Point, Silver Blue Tabby Point, Silver Chocolate Tabby Point and Silver Lilac Tabby Point. These cats lack the beige or buff colouring in the hairs making up the striped pattern, and this is replaced by a silvery version of the basic colour. They are therefore more pastel or silver in colour. So far only the Seal and Chocolate varieties have been bred and their future remains uncertain.

Most Tabby Point Siamese breeders mate the Tabby Point with a Seal, Blue, Chocolate or Lilac Point. When the breed was first being developed such 'backcrosses' were essential. Now that the type of the Tabby Points is as good as (and sometimes better than) that of the older Siamese varieties, like to like matings are quite acceptable and, if the breeder wants to produce pure-breeding Tabby Points, they are essential.

The main problems besetting Tabby Point Siamese breeders are the occurrence of cats with tails showing darker striping than in the mask, or even a different colour within the classification (for example, dark chocolate tail and milk chocolate points). And there is also the persistent prejudice of non-Tabby Point breeders against all cats bred from Tabby Point pedigrees. It says much for the Tabby Point breeders that they have persisted in their efforts despite these problems, and now that the genetics of the Tabby Point are generally better understood both problems should soon be resolved.

With the advent of Red Points and Tabby Points it was predictable that other colour combinations would follow. Already Siamese had appeared whose points were cream (the dilute of red), and inevitably there were cats with tortoiseshell points – inevitably, because in mating together a Seal Point and a Red Shorthair, the litters of the second generation might comprise Red Point males and Tortoiseshell Point females. A cross between two such cats would, according to genetic law, produce a Red Point female.

Several other colours were bred when Tabby Points were crossed with individuals of all points' colours. The result has been Chocolate Tortie Points, Lilac Tabby Points, various Tortie Tabby Points, and, in fact, Siamese cats with points of every colour and colour combination proper to the domestic cat.

It should be stressed that the cats concerned breed true; only in this way could they have obtained recognition from the governing bodies. If you mate together a male and female Tabby Point, their kittens will all be Tabby Points. The same applies to all the Siamese colours (except, of course, to the Tortie Points, which are always female). Anyone who owns a Siamese can be sure that, mated to its like, it will produce its like.

Chapter IV
The Shorthairs:
British and American

The American Shorthair

THE American Shorthairs are the descendants of the original breed of cats which was taken to North America by the early English settlers, and indeed their type is very similar to that of the resident domestic cats in Britain, which apparently arrived there with the Romans.

When the Cat Fancy started, most of the cats were unknown ancestry, and so it is difficult to trace any particular lines. But as long ago as 1900 a short-haired orange tabby was imported from England by a Miss J Cathcart. This cat, Ch Belle of Bradford, was the first short-haired cat registered by the American Cat Fanciers Association and, in spite of the name, was apparently a male.

Over the years, other imports followed and mating with the resident cats produced the variety which came to be known as the Domestic Shorthair, now called the American Shorthair. In the early days of cat shows the Persians (or Longhairs)

were the preferred breed and it took a number of years for the American Shorthairs to establish themselves as the firm favourites they are today, both with the breeders and with the general public.

There are many outstanding examples of all colours, and they are frequent winners in the National Awards given by the Cat Fanciers Association, a Tortoiseshell and a Silver Tabby being among the prizewinners for 1973/4. Not all are show specimens: many are neutered pets, much loved by their owners.

The American Shorthair is a very muscular cat with a large, full-cheeked head; the nose is medium in length, with gentle curves, while the medium-sized ears have slightly rounded tips, and the round, wide-open eyes have a slight slant to the outer apertures. The medium to large body is powerfully built with a well-developed chest and the legs are of medium length on firm, rounded paws. The tail is of medium length, being thickish at the base, with the tip having a blunt appearance. The short, thick fur is rather hard in texture.

The American Shorthair is not a cobby cat, and seen side by side with an Exotic Shorthair the difference between them is clearly marked, although the colours and

The American shorthair is very similar to the British shorthair and is descended from the original cats taken to America by the early English settlers

coat patterns recognized are practically the same for both. There are the self colours which are black, white, red and cream, the last two being comparatively rare; and there are the tabbies, both classic and mackerel, which can be silver, red, brown, blue and cream. Other varieties are the much-admired Calico (Tortoiseshell and White) and the Tortoiseshell, the Blue-Cream, with a patched rather than brindled coat (which is preferred in Britain), the Chinchilla, Shaded Silver, Smoke, Blue, and the still rare Cameos. The eye colour varies according to the coat colour, and should be copper or deep orange in all cases, except in the Chinchilla and Shaded Silver which should have green or blue-green eyes. The Silver Tabby should have green or hazel eyes. The eyes of the White, as with all white pedigree cats, whether long- or short-coated, may be deep blue, brilliant gold, or odd-eyed, having one eye of each colour. Faults are a fluffy coat, deep breaks in the nose, a kinked tail and locket or button markings.

The American Exotic Shorthair

A cat which lives up to its name is the Exotic Shorthair, combining as it does the Persian type with soft, thick fur of medium length; the result is most attractive. The variety has had a comparatively short history and was produced originally by the cross-mating of an American Shorthair with a Persian. In 1966 a Mrs Jane Martinke suggested that there should be a hybrid class for 'Domestics of mixed Persian and American Shorthair parentage', to be known as 'Exotic Shorthairs'. Originally all the short-haired cats in the USA (apart from those of foreign type, such as the Siamese and Abyssinian breeds) were considered as one class, then known as Domestic, but now known as the American Shorthair. It was found that at shows the ones with shorter noses and smaller ears invariably won, so that there was some cross-breeding between the Domestic and Persian varieties, in an attempt to produce more of prize-winning type. The resulting cats were short-haired and sturdy, but with definite Persian type. They became very popular, but also caused confusion and dissatisfaction among other breeders of American Shorthairs.

Therefore the Cat Fanciers' Association took up Mrs Martinke's suggestion and created two classes for Domestic cats and two Standards, one for the American and one for the Exotic. Breeders who thought their American Shorthairs were closer to the Exotic type could transfer their cats to this class. This has proved to be an excellent idea for classifying the Shorthairs properly, as the imported British Shorthairs, the American Domestics and the now Exotics had previously been appearing in the same class. It had proved difficult for judges to know exactly what they were looking for when judging.

Closely allied to the British Shorthair, the Exotic type is very near to that of the Persian, the nose being much shorter and more snub than that of the British Shorthair. The head of the Exotic is massive and round with full cheeks, the nose is short, snub and broad with a definite break. The ears are small and round at the tips, while the luminous eyes are large and round and of a colour which is in keeping with the coat colour. The body is cobby on short, thick legs, with large rounded paws, and the tail is short but well in proportion to the body. The fur is beautifully soft in texture, medium in length and very dense, and grooming is comparatively simple.

The colours recognized are numerous and are the same as for the Persians. They are the self colours (that is, the same colour all over) which include white, black, blue, red and cream, the Bicolour, the Blue-Cream (with patched coat, not intermingled as in Britain), and the Tabbies, with either mackerel or classic tabby markings in silver, red, brown, blue (with blue markings on a pale bluish-ivory ground colour), and cream with darker cream markings on a paler cream background. There are also the strikingly coloured Tortoiseshells and Calicos (the

The Exotic Shorthair is closely allied to the British Shorthair, although in type it bears a closer resemblance to the Persian. It is a very attractive cat and a wide variety of colours are recognized, the latest being the Cameo

latter being known as Tortoiseshell-and-White in Britain), the Chinchilla, with a pure white undercoat delicately tipped with black, as seen in the long-haired variety; the Shaded Silver, with white undercoat and the deeper black tipping forming a mantle, and the Smokes, both black and blue, with white undercoats and very deep tipping, the former with black and the latter with blue. One of the most recent groups of colours is the short-haired Cameo, in the same colours as the long-haired Cameo. These are the Shell, which is white with red tippings, the Shaded, which is white with red tipping shadings forming a mantle, the Tabby, which is off-white with red markings, and the Smoke, which has a white undercoat and deep red tippings. Faults are white lockets or buttons and kinked tails; these apply to all colours.

The Exotics are delightful cats to see and to handle. There are a number of Grand Champions, and a most striking black Smoke was one of the American Cat Fanciers' Association National Award winners for 1973/4.

Exotics are being mated to Exotics, but in all probability an occasional outcross to a Persian is necessary to keep the required type. The points awarded at shows are as follows: 30 for the head, 20 for type, 10 for the coat, 10 for condition, 20 for colour and 10 for eye colour.

British self-coloured Shorthair cats

WHEN Harrison Weir wrote the first comprehensive book on cats in 1889, the British Shorthair cat was his principal interest. Longhair cats were becoming popular, but Siamese, Abyssinian and Russian Blues were seldom seen at that time, although a few had been imported. Later all these breeds were to become much sought after but before 1895 the British self-colour Shorthair cat was first favourite. It is the opposite in appearance of the foreign Shorthair breeds which have long noses, heads and bodies. The word 'self-colour'

The Cream self-coloured Shorthair is very attractive when its coat is of an even colour, but this is a rare variety and difficult to produce without markings

means that the cat is all one colour. The Shorthairs of today are the descendants of the first domestic cats thought to have been introduced into Britain by the Romans, but careful breeding since the nineteenth century has produced short-coated cats which conform to a set standard.

British cats at their best can be described as 'square'. They should have short, sturdy bodies, short legs and tails, round heads and eyes, powerful shoulders and short necks. Noses should also be short but straight; a stop or break in the nose is not correct for the British cat. Coats should be thick and short and not too soft in texture. Ideally the British cat should not be bred with Longhairs or foreign breeds, because some of the resulting kittens will lose type.

Descendants of the British cats taken to America by the early settlers are now recognized as a breed over there by the Cat Fanciers' Association. Called Domestic Shorthairs, they are slowly growing in popularity and more and more breeders are becoming interested in them.

Sadly, the popularity of the British cat in Britain itself has declined in favour of the more exotic breeds and consequently they are in short supply. Often there is a very long waiting list for Shorthair kittens. Fortunately there are breeders who admire the British cat and we do see representatives of most colours in the cat shows. Some are never registered with the Governing Council of the Cat Fancy and turn up as magnificent neuters in Household Pet classes.

First, let us deal with the British White Shorthair. There are three variations of this lovely cat: blue-eyed, orange- or yellow-eyed and odd-eyed. The blue-eyed is rare and usually deaf; it is beautiful when the eyes are of a deep blue. The orange-eyed is very striking and occasionally deaf. It is said that if a white kitten has a dark smudge on the forehead it is not deaf; in any case the mark soon fades away. The odd-eyed variety has now been given championship status in Britain, as in America; they are useful for breeding cats with either blue or orange eyes. It is a good thing that the odd-eyed variety, Longhair and Shorthair, has now been recognized by the Governing Council of the Cat Fancy as they invariably have excellent colour in both eyes and breeders would be encouraged to keep them because they are rare. White cats need guarding from dangers on the roads because of their deafness. They

British self-coloured Shorthairs have short, sturdy bodies, round heads and eyes and powerful shoulders. Coats should be thick and short and not too soft in texture. There are three varieties of the White Shorthair (above); the Blue Shorthair (left), is also known as the British Blue; the Black (below and inset) is striking

must be kept in very clean conditions otherwise the fur, and particularly the tail, becomes yellow. This loses points in a show.

White males can be used for mating with Tortie and Whites and with Blacks; mating with Creams and Reds may produce the odd pure White and Bi-colours, which are now a recognized breed and eligible for championship status. White kittens are very pink when born but the fur soon grows and they will look enchanting.

Centuries ago white cats were said to possess magical powers and to bring luck to their owners. In fairy stories the white cat was usually the handsome prince or the beautiful princess in disguise. It is considered to be the most gentle and loving of all the British colour varieties. But in some countries it was thought to be unlucky.

Black cats are controversial. Many people prefer them to any other colour and consider them lucky; many superstitions revolve around them. In the Middle Ages the cat, which for thousands of years had been revered, became a symbol of hatred and cruelty. Black cats in particular were then said to be unlucky and were hated because they were thought to be the friends of Satan and the familiars of witches. The Black cat is thought to have a larger amount of electricity in the fur than any other breed; this causes it to crackle in frosty weather when touched and this, no doubt, caused ignorant people to fear them.

Below: the British Black has orange eyes which contrast with its sleek black coat

A British Black of good type with orange eyes, a sleek dense coat, lacking white hairs or patches, is very beautiful. Sometimes the eyes are copper-coloured and bring to mind Shakespeare's lines in 'Pericles'–'the cat with eyne of burning coal that crouches near the mouse's hole'. Sir Winston Churchill had a favourite cat, a magnificent Black called Nelson, that slept on his bed and never left him when he was at home. Black cats are fearless and independent. The females are often very small and pretty; they love their kittens and will defend them fiercely if danger threatens. You may not take liberties with a Black cat.

The breed is useful for breeding Silvers, and if paired with Reds can produce Tortoiseshells. Crossed with an orange-eyed White the Black will produce kittens of both colours. Black kittens often have brownish coats which change to dense black as they grow. The head of a Black cat adorned the posters advertising the first big cat show held at the Crystal Palace in 1871.

Years ago famous breeders bred some good specimens and many were entered for the early shows. A male and a female exhibited in 1902 were called King of the Blacks and House Cat respectively. They were unbeaten. Today we still have a few excellent representatives of the breed and several have attained the honour of 'Best Shorthair in Show'.

A Smoke will often turn up in a litter resulting from a mating between a Black and a Silver Tabby. Many years ago short-haired Smokes were a recognized breed but the variation faded out and, like

the spotted cats, has re-appeared after a lapse of many years. Not as spectacular as the long-haired Smokes, they are, however, very attractive. The top coat is black, the undercoat white, and eye colour is usually orange or copper. Breeders are pleased that the Governing Council of the Cat Fancy has given official recognition to this breed once again.

The colour variety known as the British Blue cat is so named to distinguish it from the Foreign Blue breeds. The appearance of the Blues approximates most nearly to the Blacks; they have the same sturdy bodies, round heads, full cheeks and big well-opened eyes of deep yellow or orange. The coat should be short and 'harsh' in texture, very thick, the fur across the shoulders has a 'tucked' appearance giving it a very distinctive frosty look; the tail should be short and thick. British Blues are usually very placid in temperament; the kittens are very appealing and frequently take Best in Show honours. Blues are useful for mating to Creams and Blue-Creams in particular.

The Cream cat is very attractive when the coat is unmarked and of an even pale colour. This is very hard to attain and can be achieved only by careful selective breeding. Creams are usually of excellent type and should have deep orange or copper eyes, which are a good contrast to the coat. Some good unmarked pale cats and kittens have appeared; some have heavy markings and ringed tails. In many cases the markings fade away, although rings on the tail, however faint, seem to remain. On the other hand, we have seen unmarked kittens which developed markings as they grew older. Creams are relatively rare and a good specimen usually does extremely well at shows for this reason.

This colour variety is a challenge to breeders, who hope to produce first-class specimens. They are useful for producing other colours; a Cream male mated to a Tortie or Tortie and White could sire kittens like the mother, and perhaps a self-White mated to a British Blue female could result in Blue males and Blue-Cream females. Mated to a Blue-Cream, the resultant kittens could be Blue males, Blue-Cream females or male and female Creams. Variety is the spice of life and, if breeders will take care to use Creams and Blue-Creams with the palest coats, they can breed outstanding kittens.

British Shorthair cats when healthy are easy to rear and care for. Although they should not be left out of doors in bad weather, they do not like over-heated conditions. They should be groomed daily with a fine comb and their coat polished with a piece of silk or preferably hand groomed. Ears and teeth should be inspected regularly.

The British Shorthair Spotted cat

WHEN a judge at a cat show is presented with a class of British Shorthair Spotted cats, the first thing he looks for is good and clearly spotted markings, well formed and quite distinct from the background colouration of the coat. All other characteristics of the breed are of only secondary importance to these markings.

As in the various species of spotted wild cats in which the spotted pattern reaches its peak, there are various kinds of spotting in the domestic cat. Some cats have a great many small, round spots; some have large, randomly placed spots; some spots are oval, some oblong and some rosette-shaped. Any of these markings may be of equal merit however, as long as they are quite clearly defined and do not run into each other to give the appearance of broken mackerel-tabby bars. The spots may be of any colour suitable to the ground colouration of the cat's fur, and the fewer striped markings, that are found on legs and chest, the better.

If judging is strictly by points at a cat show, the judge will allocate seventy-five per cent of his marks for the spotted pattern and the remaining twenty-five per cent for the other characteristics which are the same as desired for any other British short-haired variety. The large, round head with its full cheeks, small, rounded ears and large, round, lustrous eyes are typical of the breed, as is the close-knit, cobby body, with its short, sturdy legs and short, thick tail.

Spotted cats have been depicted in works of art for centuries, on Egyptian scrolls, Roman mosaics and in various paintings, and these are very like the present-day 'Spotties' both in conformation and in markings. The breed was extremely popular around 1880, attractively marked kittens being retained from litters and eventually making feline history when a first prize was taken at the Crystal Palace Cat Show by a lovely spotted hybrid, the product of a mating between a domestic tabby and a Scottish Wild Cat. Because their distinctive spotted markings resemble those of many wild cats, it has been said that the oldest domestic cats known were spotted. Although spotted cats were exhibited at the early cat shows of the nineteenth century, they were virtually unknown for many years, appearing only as the result of chance matings. It was not until 1960 that a definite breeding programme was established. Some outstand-

The Spotted cat has a spotted coat, but tabby markings are allowed on the head

ing Spotties were produced by mating Silver Tabbies with Black Shorthairs.

With the importation of more exotic cats, such as the Siamese and Angora or Persian, which filled the classes at the newly instituted cats shows of the era, the spotted cats lost favour, and these, along with the other types of tabby, gradually faded into obscurity. It is only in the last few years that a few dedicated and enthusiastic breeders decided to revive the old breed. By judicious matings and carefully drawn-up breeding programmes they have succeeded admirably. Today, although never seen in great numbers, Spotted British Shorthairs are being bred well up to the required standard and in several colour varieties, and are often to be seen in the final line-up for the Best in Show awards. One magnificent Brown Spotted male, Brynbuboo Bosselot achieved the coveted Grand Champion title in Britain in 1973, a tribute to the breeding skill and selection of his owner.

Owners of British 'Spotties' declare them to be the most loving and undemanding cats they have ever owned. They are very easy to maintain in the peak of condition with the minimum of grooming. A thorough brushing and combing every few days to remove loose hair, and a

Clearly defined spots, essential if the Breed Standard is to be observed, are evident in this beautiful Silver variety

weekly inspection of the ears, between the pads and through the coat for signs of parasitic infestation, is all they need. For show purposes give a hot bran bath, or a dry shampoo with a special powder made specifically for the cleansing of cats' fur, and when the coat is free from grease and dust, thoroughly brush it clean. A little witch hazel or coat dressing may be applied to the palms of the hands and then smoothed down the coat to give an added sparkle before a final rub-down with a chamois leather or silk scarf. But remember that no powder or application of any other substance is allowed in the show hall. There must be no plucking or trimming of the coat, and no artificial colouring or other preparation may be applied to the fur, or the exhibit may be disqualified.

Spotties enjoy cat shows and are not upset or stressed by their day out. They love the admiration of the crowds of visitors and, after the judging, usually curl up and sleep the afternoon away, quite unconcerned by the bustle about them. They mature early, having their first oestrous period at about seven months, but are usually not mated until the second period, so that they have attained full maturity and the age of about one year before any kittens are born. An average litter contains three or four good-sized kittens which may be spotted or of some other pattern, depending upon the genetic

make-up of the stud male used for mating. If a suitable Spotted stud is not to be found, top quality British Black or British Blue males may be used, but they may or may not carry the modification gene required to produce the spotted pattern. Sometimes, therefore, spotted mother cats produce classic Tabby, Smoke or even self-coloured kittens.

The kittens are born after a gestation period of 63 to 67 days. Provide the queen with a dark, warm box in a quiet place in which to give birth. The actual delivery is usually fairly long, but without incident, and the kittens are contented and quiet from birth. Spotted cats make excellent mothers, feeding and cleaning the litter until the crawling stage, then teaching the kittens to eat solids, use their toilet tray and the scratching post. They are easy to feed and should have a well-balanced, varied diet, and plenty of milk. Fresh water should be available to them at all times, and lumps of raw meat fed once or twice weekly to help keep teeth and gums in good condition.

Spotted cats do not thrive as totally indoor cats, and make better pets when they can have free range of a home, with a garden in which they can exercise and hunt. But, because of its liking for the free-range life, the Spotted cat is more likely to present its owner with problems that do not arise with the hearth-and-home loving breeds.

The custom of some owners of fitting their cat with a collar is not to be recommended for the Spotted variety. Cats get into some very strange situations in the course of their hunting lives, and in many of these situations the collar can be a hindrance, if not a distinct liability. Tree-climbing is an obvious example of the type of activity that can result in trouble for your 'Spottie' if it is fitted with a collar. It is not unknown for a cat to be caught by its collar on a stout twig or branch, and to hang there for several hours until it was seen and rescued. But supposing this had happened in the depths of a wood?

The only reason for fitting a cat with a collar should be when you want the cat on a lead. Some cats like to go for a walk with their owners and, if this walk takes place along busy roads, then a lead is advisable. So, in these circumstances, fit your cat with one of those collars that have an elastic section: the stretchy elastic will prevent it from being choked. Choose a collar of medium width, for if it is too thin it will cut into the neck and if too wide it will most certainly cause chafing and a sore spot. As to the choice of material, leather is to be preferred to man-made substitutes such as plastic. And in choosing the clip to link

collar and lead, try to buy the kind that slides open rather than the spring type. Spring clips have been known to fasten on to a cat's ear, and releasing the clip means momentarily increasing the pain to the animal.

Undoubtedly, the owner of a Spotted Shorthair will find that his cat is a determined bird hunter. This habit causes the humane owner much unease, and yet there is little or nothing that can be done to improve matters. Some owners profess to have cured their cats of the bird-catching habit by using a number of ploys. One will fit his cat with a bell that hangs from a collar, but collars are not recommended for reasons already given. And some cats are clever enough to hunt without causing the bell to tinkle! Other owners have tried a method used with dogs—that of hanging the dead bird round the animal's neck. But it has never proved wholly successful.

There is only one way out of this impasse, and that is for the owner to change his attitude towards bird-catching and to let it continue without hindrance. This may seem a very unkind and even cruel attitude to adopt, yet consider what you are doing by interfering. Firstly, you are trying to rewrite one of the laws of Nature. The domestic cat is descended

Although Blue Spotted cats like this are now seen more at shows, they are still less popular than the Silvers

from cats that stalked in the wild, and they have inherited an instinct to hunt. You may be successful in training a pet dog not to catch birds but it is unlikely you will ever train a cat to refute its natural instincts in this way. Dogs are much more subservient to man than cats; cats give their loyalty to their owners while retaining their independence.

Punishment, too, often produces something not intended. You may make the cat confused; it does not know whether you are punishing it for bringing the bird to the house, or perhaps for not catching a bigger bird. Attempting to thwart your cat's natural instincts will produce frustration in the animal, and who wants a neurotic cat?

The Silver variety of 'Spottie' looks very attractive on a background of green lawn, and with its jet black spots on a silver base colour, when moving through the shrubbery, it resembles a miniature snow-leopard. This variety appears to be the most popular today, although the Brown and Blue are also being produced in fair numbers and are appearing more and more on the show bench.

The British Shorthair Tabby

TABBY cats come in all colours, shapes and sizes, from the pedigree aristocrat to the 'Tiger on the Hearth', as the household pet is sometimes called. The coat pattern, described as marbled, is the oldest type known and is shared by the Scottish wild cat and, of course, by the tiger itself. It is thought that all domestic cats originally had tabby markings, and if all the domestic cats throughout the world were allowed to inter-mate, the likely result would be that all cats would be tabby.

The origin of the word 'tabby' is interesting, for, according to the dictionary, it derived from a type of ribbed silk or taffeta originating in a district of old Baghdad called Attabiya. The silk was much used in the seventeenth century and, when watered by a special process, became covered with wavy lines, often being described as 'tabby' cloth.

There are many variations of tabby markings: the more usual are known as 'blotched' or 'classic', while a flecked coat is called 'Mackerel', and a spotted coat is a 'Spotted', or 'Spottie'. The classic pattern of markings has swirls round the cheeks,

127

delicate lines running down the face, 'spectacle' markings round the eyes, and a mark like an 'M' on the forehead. There should be two 'necklaces' round the neck, which are often called the 'mayoral chains'. Three dark stripes should run down the spine, with the flanks and saddle having thick bands of contrasting colour, which resemble a butterfly when looked at from above. The tail and legs should be ringed. All these markings should be completely separate, not blurred or brindled.

On the show bench the colour and markings must be as near perfect as possible to conform with the Standard laid down by the specialist Club and upheld by the Governing Council of the Cat Fancy. The Shorthair Silver Tabby, perhaps the most spectacular of all the colours, should have a coat of pure silver-grey (not white), with dense black markings; the tail should be ringed and the neck rings unbroken. When the nose is brick-red, the eyes should be green; when black, the eyes are usually hazel.

Silver Tabbies are quiet and reserved, very affectionate but not demonstrative. They have pretty, smiling faces and are sometimes inclined to be shy, not always fond of being handled, but seldom difficult. Good breeders, they mix well with other cats, provided they are introduced as kittens. They are good parents and litters average four or five kittens. Their tendency to show brown on the nose and paws is

Previous page: the Shorthair Red Tabby should have no white on its coat. Right: an example of the Brown Shorthair Tabby; (below) a Silver Shorthair Tabby

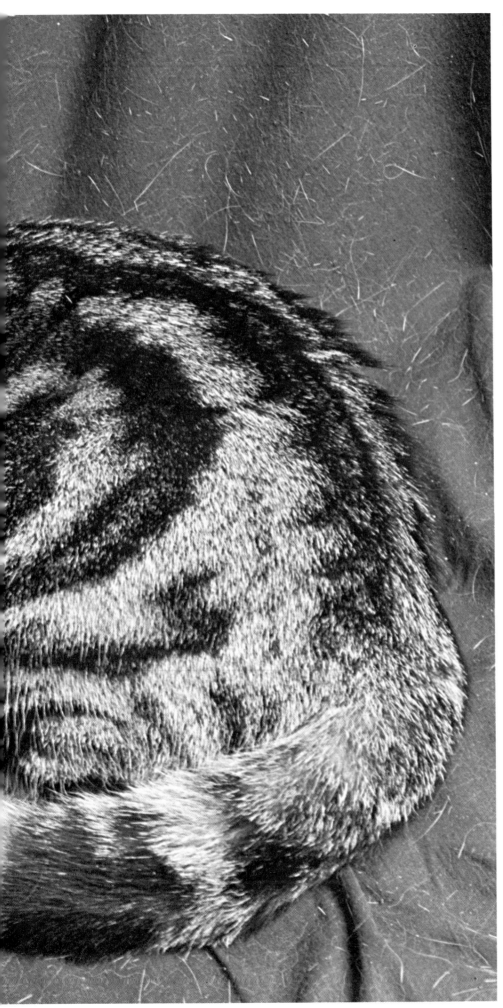

judged a fault, but if Silver is bred to Silver, introducing an occasional Black, all should be well. The Silver Tabby has long been the most popular of the three colours, and many were registered in the first Cat Register, published in 1898, under such names as Sweet Angelus, Silver Bangle, Sweet Briar, Silver Chieftain, the Grey Lady, and Moonshine, all of which suit the Silver very well. In those days the usual prices to pay for such cats were between £25 to £100.

The Shorthair Red Tabby is very spectacular, with a rich red ground colour and markings of a darker red; eyes should be orange or hazel. No white in the coat is permissible. This colour tabby must not, of course, be confused with the so-called ginger cat, whose coat is much paler and often shows white on chin, chest and tip of tail. The Red Tabby is not shy and, in fact, may be a little fiery at times, as befits its colour. Males can be very large and handsome. Females are not prolific breeders, but make good mothers.

The males of the Brown Tabby can be massive when fully grown. The ground colour of the coat should be rich sable or brown, with black markings. No white should appear anywhere, although this ideal is difficult to attain today, so that few really outstanding Browns are seen in shows. It is rare to find a Brown Tabby without a light chin. Eye colour may be more varied than that of Silvers and Reds – either orange, yellow or green. Brown Tabbies have benevolent expressions, the males with their heavy neck rings looking dignified and somewhat aloof, the females small and placid. Like the other colours they are affectionate, loyal and companionable.

Mackerel Tabbies are so called because their coat pattern resembles the fish of that name. They are rare and may be seen in classes with cats of the marbled pattern if colour, type and so forth conform. They must not be confused with the Spotted cats, which have their own Standard of Points and their own classes.

Cream and Blue Tabbies are occasionally seen. The Creams often have very distinct markings of light red on a cream ground, and their eyes are usually copper or deep orange. The Blues have coats of good colour, but their markings are not as distinct. These colours are not yet recognized by the Governing Council, but both these and Cameo are recognized in the United States, as well as the Browns, Reds and Silvers of Britain.

The British Shorthair Tabby is brave and resourceful. There are many stories of the ways they have warned their owners of danger and of their tenacity in defending their kittens. With the exception of the Siamese, they will endure more privation than any other breed of cat.

Shorthair Tortoiseshells

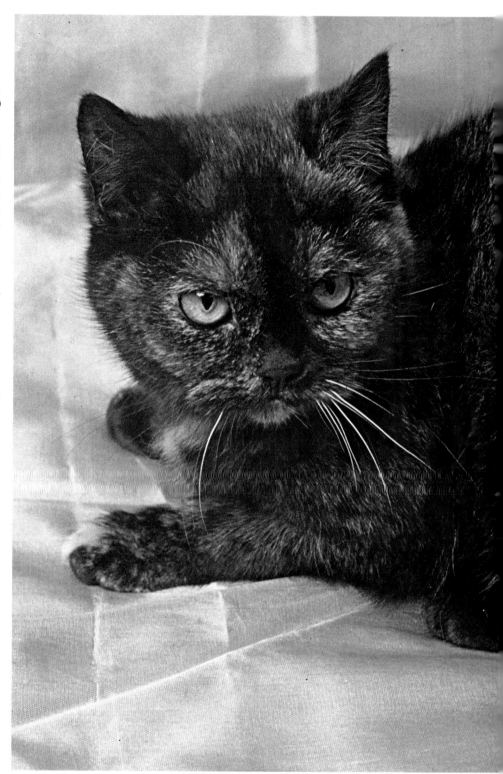

TWO cat breeds with almost identical genetic make-up are the Tortoiseshell, and the Tortoiseshell-and-White British Shorthairs. These cats are almost invariably female, and the odd few males which do turn up in litters from time to time generally prove to be infertile. This means, therefore, that Tortoiseshell and Tortoiseshell-and-White queens are mated to self-coloured stud cats, usually Black, Red or Cream, and the percentage of kittens born like their mothers is very low. This poses enormous problems for breeders of show stock hoping to meet the high standards set by the Governing Council of the Cat Fancy.

When a Tortoiseshell female is mated to a Black male, her litter will consist of Black males and females, Red males and Tortoiseshell females, the number of each depending solely on chance. When mated to a Red male she may have Black males and females, Red males and females, and Tortoiseshell females. When both queen and stud carry the gene which modifies black to blue, even more possibilities occur, for the litter may have males which are Black, Blue, Red or Cream, and females which are Black, Blue Tortoiseshell or Blue-Cream. If the stud cat is Red or Cream, carrying this blue gene, there is the additional possibility of Red and Cream females. These remarks also apply to the Tortoiseshell-and-White, with the addition of white markings.

In both varieties, the Standard of points calls for normal British type, including well-knit, cobby body structure; short, sturdy legs; short, blunt tail; round, full-cheeked face with small, rounded ears and large round eyes of copper, deep orange or hazel. Striking examples of the breeds may have the desired red or black blaze running down the nose and bisecting the face, but this is not essential. The Tortoiseshell must have a brightly patched coat of black, light red and dark red, and will be penalized if the red patches show any tabby markings or white hairs. The Tortoiseshell-and-White has additional white areas, and these cats are even more difficult to breed to the Standard, most kittens having too much white, and lacking coloured patches on the legs. Black-and-White and Red-and-White bicolour males

Tortoiseshell and Tortoiseshell-and-White cats are generally female, because sex and colour are genetically linked

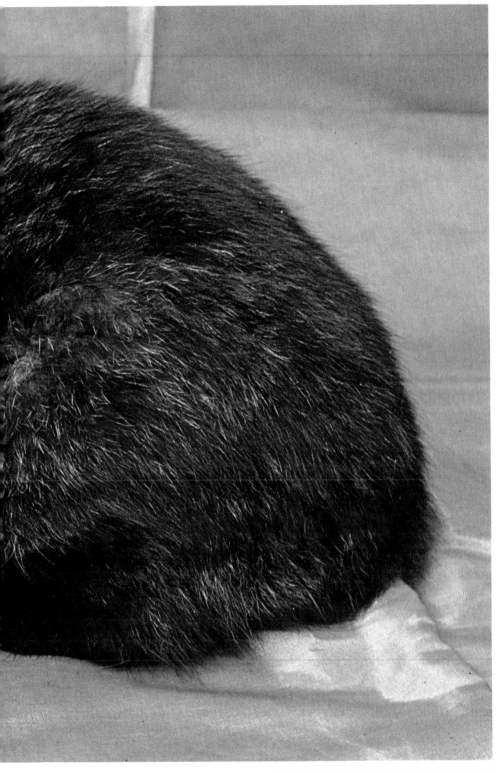

have been used in breeding programmes recently, however, and this policy has resulted in some magnificently marked progeny appearing on the show benches.

Although among the oldest of the British breeds, very few records are available of the history of these cats, but it is known that a Tortoiseshell was exhibited at the Crystal Palace Cat Show in 1871, and at the turn of the century some males were produced. The 1900 to 1905 stud book of the National Cat Club lists two Tortoiseshell males as having won championships: Lady Rachel Alexander's Ballochmyle Samson and Mrs Herring's King Saul, both of which apparently sired kittens. Lady Alexander also bred a male Tortoiseshell-and-White, called Ballochmyle Bachelor, which was exhibited at the Crystal Palace Show in 1912, and shown extensively until 1914, but there are no records of progeny from this aptly named fellow.

Tortoiseshell cats are usually very affectionate and make wonderful house pets when spayed. They have quiet and gentle natures and make excellent mothers, giving birth easily but liking complete privacy while it is taking place. The Tortoiseshell-and-White, once known in England as the Spanish Cat, and called the Calico Cat in the U.S.A., has a rather stronger personality on the whole, being slightly more extrovert. Both types are excellent mousers, and their mongrel equivalents may be seen in large numbers on British farms, where they are welcomed for keeping vermin in check.

Basically very healthy and hardy, these cats are easy to keep in peak condition by feeding a good, well-balanced diet including a proportion of fresh raw meat. Because of their hunting habits, they need to be dosed every four months against parasitic worms, and their coats must be inspected regularly for signs of external parasites which they may have picked up from rats, mice and voles. Their short, dense coats are easily maintained in good order by brushing firmly and finishing off with a silk scarf or chamois leather. The tricolours can have their white parts spruced up before a show with a special feline dry-shampoo, worked well in with the fingertips, allowed to do its cleansing and then brushed thoroughly out again. The coloured areas of the coat are made to sparkle by the application of a little witch hazel to the palms of the hands, which are rubbed together and then slicked down the coat before the final rub down with the chamois leather. The ears must be scrupulously clean and the eyes bright and free from discharge.

Kept reasonably warm, but not in overheated or stuffy conditions, both varieties appear very resistant to upper respiratory infections and gastric upsets.

Two-colour British Shorthairs

THE Blue-Cream cat is a comparatively rare breed of British Shorthair, due to the sex-linkage factor which means that virtually all of them are female. The breed, which first appeared on the show benches in 1951, captivated all who saw it, and went from strength to strength, eventually achieving a breed number and full recognition with Championship status in 1956.

Ethereal in appearance, the Blue-Creams in Britain and throughout Europe have softly intermingled coats of pastel blue and pale cream, giving the overall effect of shot-silk. A cream blaze is permissible and the eye colour may be copper, orange or yellow. In Canada and the USA the Standard differs considerably, and calls for

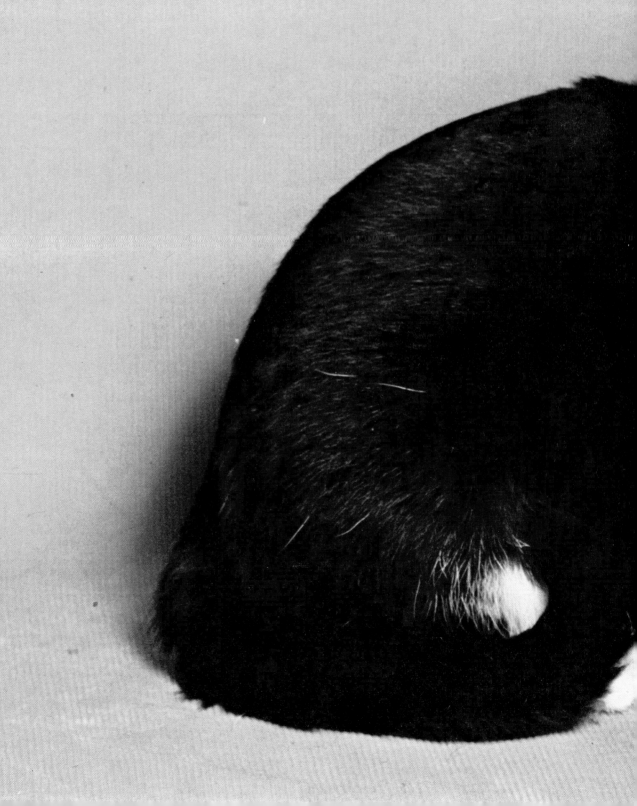

a distinctly blue cat with well-defined patches of cream, and with the eye colour being only a brilliant gold. However, all Standards deplore any sign of tabby markings or white hairs.

Less massively built than the British Blue, the Blue-Cream nevertheless has superb type, and credit for this should be given to the breed's pioneers and their careful selection of foundation breeding stock. This breed is typically British with a good depth of body, full and broad chest; thick, well-set tail; sturdy legs with neat, well-rounded feet; a broad head with well-developed cheeks; small, slightly rounded ears with good width between; and large, lustrous, well-opened round eyes. The British Standard awards 40 points for type, 35 points for colour, and 20 points for the eyes, which may be any of the colours mentioned above, but under no circumstances is green acceptable.

The coat texture of a Blue-Cream is very important. It must be short and fine, and never coarse or hard to the touch. Hand-grooming will keep the Blue-Cream in top condition, but the coat may need extra attention during moulting periods, when a very fine toothed comb should be used to remove all the dead hairs as they loosen;

Bicoloured cats such as this Black-and-White were once called Magpie cats

The Manx

THE Manx is a tailless cat with a mysterious origin. Legend has it that the Phoenician traders brought the tailless cat from Japan, and this may well be correct, for there have been repeated reports of tailless cats in the East. Another story, and that most readily accepted by British fanciers, is that the breed originated in the Isle of Man. This story is now disputed by many authors, who claim that the Manx arrived on the Isle of Man when a Spanish ship, on which these cats lived, foundered and sank just off the island. The tailless cat survivors are said to have swum ashore and bred with the native cat population. In fact, anyone who owns a Manx will soon become aware of this breed's inherent love of water. The

double coat of the breed, typical of many animals which inhabit the tropical islands of the Malayan Archipelago, lends support to the theory that the Manx originated in this part of the world. Many ships from Malaya were in action during the wars involving the Spanish Armada, and the Manx cats could easily have been aboard them until some of them reached the Isle of Man.

Whatever its origin, the Manx is indisputably an ancient and fascinating breed. According to a writer of 1900, 'the Manx is considered by many people as a natural curiosity. It differs from the ordinary cat but little, except in the absence of a tail or even an apology for one. The hind legs are thicker and rather longer than the

ordinary cat's and it runs more like a hare'. The writer goes on to state: 'the Manx cat came from the Isle of Man originally and is a distinct breed'. The description of the Manx in this account was illustrated by a picture of Pan, a blue-eyed white Manx owned by Miss Hester Cochran of Wimborne, England. The Manx was very popular with the cat lovers of that era.

Knowledgeable breeders will disagree with the statement that the Manx differs little from the ordinary domestic cat, for it has a shorter back, longer hind legs,

It is not only the lack of a tail, but also its longer hind legs, that distinguishes the Manx from other breeds

137

New breeds of Shorthair cat

THE pedigree short-haired cat breeds can most easily be divided into three groups: first, those with massive, cobby shape and build known as British Shorthairs; secondly, those with finer bone known as the Foreign Shorthairs; and lastly, those with the shape and build of the Siamese that are usually described as the Orientals.

Within each group the whole range of cat colours and coat patterns may exist. In rare instances, other differences occur, a notable example being that of the Rex breeds. These were developed from cats with a mutation factor giving them wavy coats. Two mutants were found in the early 1960s, both in England. Since that date other mutations have occurred and at present three types of rex coat are identified – Cornish Rex, Devon Rex and Oregon Rex.

Other new breeds produced by characteristics quite new to the domestic cat are the Wirehair, the Japanese Bobtail and the Scottish Fold. The Wirehair is bred and exhibited both in the USA and in Europe. Its name is fully descriptive; the wire-haired effect is produced by a gene removing the soft underhair and making the guard hairs more wiry. The Japanese Bobtail is a cat of semi-foreign type, bred

Inset, (top): Lavender is one of a new range of Oriental cat colours recently produced in Britain. The Foreign White (centre) is identical to the Siamese except for its pure white coat. The Scottish Fold (below) has unusual folded ears

in self red, black or white and tortie-and-white coat colours. It has a bobbed, and often knobbly tail. Like the Wirehair, the Japanese Bobtail is not yet exhibited in Britain. The Scottish Fold is a native of Britain, first seen in Scotland in 1961. It is a cat of British type or conformation, with ears folded over at the apex like those of a young puppy. Many have short, blunt-ended tails. The variety has not yet been granted recognition by the Governing Council of the Cat Fancy.

New varieties produced by combinations of coat colour and pattern already in existence in other breeds include two beautiful British Shorthair varieties, the Smoke and the Chinchilla. These two varieties are allied genetically, but have two quite separate pedigree lines. Another beautiful but rare British variety is the Blue Cream and White. Other new British coat colours and patterns include Chocolate, Lilac and Chocolate Tabby.

Within the Foreign classification, the most notable newcomers are probably the Red, Cream, Tortie, Chocolate and Lilac Burmese, developed to become almost entirely 'Self' – that is, of one colour only and almost entirely free from tabby markings. In red breeds this is a rare achievement. The Chocolate and Lilac Burmese bred in Britain come from stock imported from the United States of America where the Chocolate is known as the Champagne. The Abyssinian is another Foreign breed in which new colours are being produced. Among them are a range of biscuit-fawn colours considered by most experts to be the equivalent of Lilac Tabby. One of the most spectacular new Abyssinian varieties is the Silver, often seen in Any Other Variety classes at shows. Another interesting new Abyssinian colour is the Blue. There will be a great number of additional combinations possible when the pedigrees of the Silvers, Blues and Creams are combined. The Russian breed is generally recognized as Blue, but one breeder is producing cats of Russian type with black or white coats. Numbers are few but the whites, in particular, have been quite successful in Any Other Variety classes at cat shows.

The Oriental group of breeds has the largest number of new varieties. Foremost among these are the Foreign Whites, cats that are Siamese in every way except colour, which is pure glistening white These cats usually produce some ordinary Siamese in each litter, but they are not classed with Siamese for exhibition purposes. Breeding Foreign Whites is an absorbing hobby, for their white coats are inherited as the result of a dominant gene whose effect is to mask all the other colours and patterns present.

In more recent years, cats with another type of white coat have been bred in Britain from stock imported from America. These white cats are similar to the Foreign Whites, having Siamese-type white coats and blue eyes, but when bred to Siamese none of the kittens will be white. Only when the kittens are bred to each other will a proportion of these other Foreign Whites appear.

Another new range of Oriental Shorthairs has sprung from an accidental mating between a Chinchilla Persian and a Chocolate Point Siamese. A study of the manner in which the colours and patterns appear in kittens of successive litters has shown that a whole new range of Oriental cat colours are possible. Those seen at cat shows to date are the Apricot Oriental Smoke, the Black Oriental Smoke, the Ivory Oriental Smoke and the Chocolate Oriental Pastel. The cats are bred in ten colours and are classified as Smoke, Silver and Pastel Groups, making thirty new varieties in all. The other colours are Blue, Lavender, Dapple Black, Dapple Blue, Dapple Chocolate, Dapple Lavender and Dapple Silver. The Oriental Smokes are Siamese-type cats with pale undercoats, and guard hairs shaded with colour. The Oriental Silvers are tabby cats with the tabby pattern in colour upon a silvery background, and have their equivalent in the Silver Tabby of other breeds.

Another Shorthair variety new to Britain, although already bred and exhibited successfully in the USA and Canada, is the Korat. This pretty little cat is of Foreign rather than Oriental type, with a shining blue-grey coat. It is different in type from the Oriental Blues. It is hoped that the British Cat Fancy will follow America and Canada and give the breed the right to compete for Championship honours in this country.

The Korat has already been successfully shown in Canada and the USA and it is now recognized in Britain.